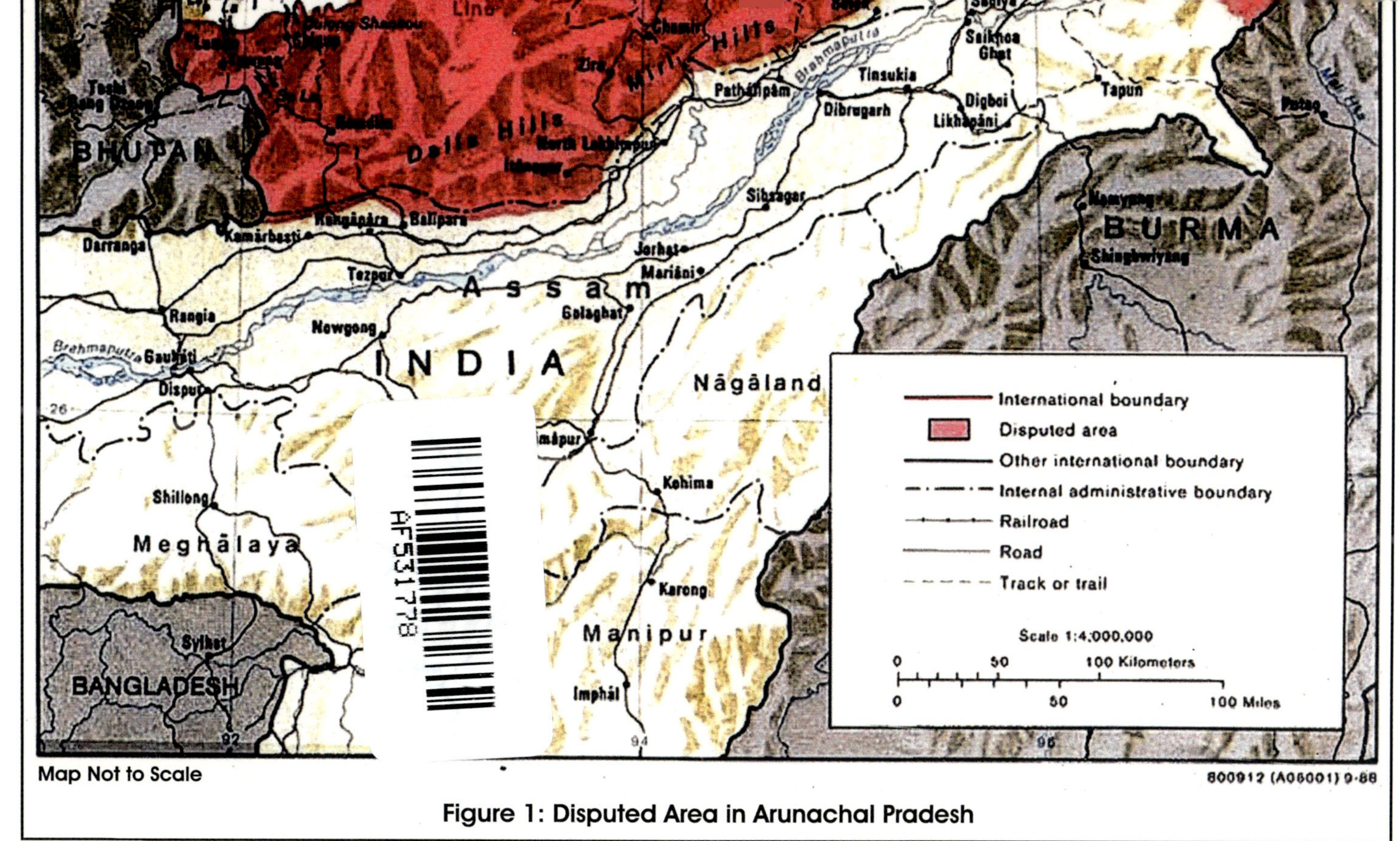


Map Not to Scale

800912 (A06001) 9-88

Figure 1: Disputed Area in Arunachal Pradesh

# India's China
# Strategic Perspectives

BY THE SAME AUTHOR

*Ayodhya Ram Temple and Hindu Renaissance*

*Economic Development and Reforms in India and China*

*Hindus Under Siege: The Way Out*

*Sri Lanka in Crisis: India's Options*

*Terrorism in India: A Strategy of Deterrence for India's National Security*

*Rama Setu: Symbol of National Unity*

*Corruption and Corporate Governance in India: Satyam, Spectrum and Sundaram*

*Hindutva and National Renaissance*

*Virat Hindu Identity: Concept and its Power*

*Building the Sri Rama Temple in Ayodhya*

*2G Spectrum Scam*

*The Ideology of India's Modern Right*

# India's China Strategic Perspectives

Subramanian Swamy, Ph.D. (Harvard)

*Member of Parliament, India*
*Former Union Cabinet Minister for Commerce, Law & Justice, India*

HAR-ANAND
PUBLICATIONS PVT LTD

**Reprint, 2025**



Published by Ashok Gosain and Ashish Gosain for
HAR-ANAND PUBLICATIONS PVT LTD
E-49/3, Okhla Industrial Area, Phase-II, New Delhi-110020
Tel: 41603490
E-mail: info@haranandbooks.com/haranand@rediffmail.com
Shop online at: www.haranandbooks.com

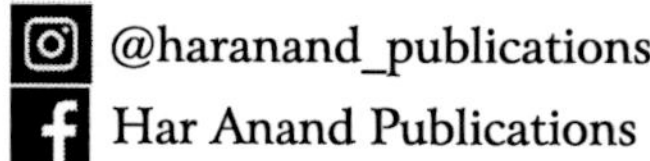


Printed in India at Megha Enterprises

# PREFACE

The perspectives in India on China today fluctuate from, at one end, China as an aggressive and expansionist threat, to the other extreme, of China as a sister ancient civilization.

This pendulum like swing perspective in moods in Indian public opinion is frequently influenced by media reports from"unfriendliness" and "perfidy", to alternatively of 'warm gestures' bordering in cultural euphoria, causing thus unstable cyclic movements in Indian policy towards China, which sows confusion in China as well, and thus destabilizes our relations with that country.

Cooperative competitiveness in world affairs as a concept has eluded Indian policy makers since the personalized foreign policy making of India's constitutional Prime Minister after British imperialist departure, viz., Jawaharlal Nehru became the irrational norm of succeeding Prime Ministers.

I propose, therefore, to argue that the first requirement of an effective Indian policy towards China is to build a national consensus on how we define our complex of interests vis-a-vis China, in a world that has dramatically changed for India since the year of the humiliating border conflict in 1962 with China.

China's negative perceptions of India, even today, is that the 1962 armed conflict was the result of Indian unreasonableness; that India wanted to inherit the ill-gotten concessions obtained by British Imperialists from the then weak China; that India is not reconciled to the situation in Tibet notwithstanding recognizing by a formal treaty twice, first 1956 and then in 2003, that Tibet is an autonomous region of China; and that India is seeking domination of South Asia, and that India is deliberately using the "myth" of a Chinese threat to find a pretext for its nuclear pursuit in defiance of the formed international opinion on disarmament, and is stirring instead to become thus a global power with the patronage of the US, which super power is seen as increasingly developing alternative options to contain China.

In the new millennium of the 21st century, there is however a substantial economic gap between China and India but it, this study concludes, is as if India were to concentrate on producing a significantly accelerated growth in agriculture, information technology, services, and exports during the next decades post 2019, the gap with China can be quickly bridged because of the current plateauing of Chinese growth rates.

Clearly, India will have to make strenuous efforts fiscally, to raise the rate of investment to reach beyond 36 per cent of GDP as a minimum condition for commencing on closing the China-India gap.

The task of course is within reach and it is a target for which the Indian people would be willing to make sacrifice. "Catching up with China" is a worthwhile slogan for India's new millennium, along with a national commitment to another goal of GDP growth at 10 per cent per year. Both goals are feasible and attainable, within India's grasp and at a striking distance. The only question is whether the Indian policy makers are upto it.

Thus, whether or not India becomes a global power in the 21st century depends on India alone and that would require in the country a combination of political unity, economic growth, social cohesion, credible military capability and shrewd diplomacy.

It is not a status anybody can then deny India. But by the same token, no power is going to confer that status on India until then. Thus, if in the years ahead, India fails to attain global status, it will be due to its domestic and diplomatic failures and not due to any international perfidy or lack of international support. Such a global status it is argued here, would have a multiplier effect if India is also able to harmonize its interest with China and manage to live in peace with dignity. The question is how such a harmonization can come about.

To do that, India thus has to define its perspective on China with clarity and transparency: Does India want a compact with China in the twenty-first century (Choice I), or does India want to participate in the growing prospect to contain China (Choice II): Or is there a third alternative of a Global Triumvirate (Choice III)?

A China-India compact, of nearly 36 per cent of the world's population, would not only after the strategic map of the world, but offer unique economic opportunities for joint ventures under the WTO disciplines especially in textiles, services and information technology.

A China-India joint supervision of the Malacca Straits would impact on nearly 75 per cent of the world's commercial sea traffic. Such a compact has thus multi-dimensional possibilities, but it is not easy to effect it. It is however not impossible. It depends on the astuteness of leadership to be able to understand and accommodate the China perspectives, and calibrated, without causing alarm in the world's present day sole super power, the USA.

New Delhi (India) SUBRAMANIAN SWAMY
January 2019

# CONTENTS

# CHAPTER 1

# The Historical Perspective

## I

It is generally accepted that contacts between Indian and China began as early as the China's Chou Dynasty and India's Gupta Dynasty (For correct date use 400 B.C.). Former Ambassador to China and a scholar of Indian history, K.M. Panikkar has written extensively but unacknowledged by "sarkari" historians on the subject, We have drawn heavily on his materials in this chapter.

Trade and commerce as also cultural contacts flourished for centuries between the two countries via the Silk Road. The most significant and lasting consequence of the contacts was the establishment of Buddhism in China. The Chinese had responded with great enthusiasm to the arrival of Buddhist missionaries and thereafter initiated steps to bring Indian Buddhist monks and scholars to help teach, explain, and to establish Buddhism firmly in China.

During the fourth and fifth centuries A.D., a second wave of Buddhist Indian monks as missionaries to China, created a counter wave of Chinese Buddhists to India for advanced training. Kumarajiva and Bodhidharma, who went from India to China, and Fa Hsien and Yuan Chuang, who came from China to India, are 'four familiar names who greatly enriched the knowledge and understanding of their countries of origin to their hosts. Bodhidharma taught Dhyana Buddhism and

Wu Shih martial arts in Shao Lin, which Japan later adopted via China as Zen Buddhism and Karate.

The dominance and firm grip that Buddhism came to acquire in China was of course the result of a long-lasting process of considerable interaction and exchange with India spread over centuries, which benefited both countries in many ways. The Chinese were responsible for preserving many valuable Sanskrit works of the Gupta and post-Gupta period, as recent excavations in Xinjiang have revealed important manuscripts, and by organizing Chinese translations of them and printing them for posterity spread the teachings of Buddha within China. Indian monks, apart from the development of religion and philosophy, promoted the advancement of astronomy, medicine, chemistry and physical exercise in China. More on this in later paragraphs.

From 1840 onwards, when most of India had come under British control, the British recruited a large number of Indians to carry out soldiering and guard duties to serve their interests in China. However, during the course of the T'aiping Rebellion, which lasted from 1850 to 1864, many Indian soldiers had been captured by the T'aipings in battle and were converted to their cause.

Almost seven decades later, this phenomenon was to be repeated when Indian soldiers and policemen in China, motivated by the struggle against imperialism, once again turned their arms against the British. This turnaround in their political loyalties and their radicalisation came about with the work of the Ghadar Party in China, and indeed, in retrospect, the Ghadar movement should figure in the history of India-China interaction as a notable chapter of "revolutionary comradeship."

The exploitation and domination by the imperialist and colonial powers that India and China experienced, and their struggles against them, did not however bring the two countries together because even though in 1947, India won her freedom from the British, and in 1949, the Communist Party of China (CPC) won the civil war and came to power in the newly proclaimed People's Republic of China, the world in which India awoke "to Independence, democracy, and freedom," China achieved "liberation" from its own Kuomintang rule. The globe post-World War II was sharply divided into two ideologically opposed blocs: the socialist and anti-West bloc led by the USSR versus the democratic anti-Communist bloc led by the United States.

Whereas the People's Republic of China was unambiguously aligned with the former, Jawaharlal Nehru, the post-1947 Prime Minister of independent India was troubled by the bi-polar world order, and equivocated, while ultimately tilting or leaning to the USSR led bloc, in the crucial hours of moral emergencies such as in Hungary in 1956. His daughter, Mrs Indira Gandhi followed the same policy of tilt, without being a formal camp-follower, towards the USSR. In Czechoslovakia in 1968, Mrs Gandhi capitulated as her father had in Hungary, and three years later in 1971, she went further signed the Indo-Soviet Treaty which required India to consult the USSR prior to reacting to any threat, and to render assistance if either's interests were threatened as it was in 1979 when China attacked Soviet ally Vietnam. In the meantime by 1960, China had broken with the USSR, and gradually entered a strategic understanding with USA.

## II

Sociologists use the term "Sanskritization" to mean the acceptance and assimilation, by Indian society, of ideas, institution and morals which were originally articulated in Sanskrit literature in India, i.e., the "cultural borrowing" of the whole complex of inter-relationship between man with himself and with the rest of the world, as well 'as the concept of the soul and its reincarnation.

China was "Sanskritized" thus for over 2000 years, and we have that on the authority of the eminent diplomat and historian Professor Hu Shih. Hu however did not look upon this "cultural domination" with favour. In Harvard's Tricentennial Celebrations Address, as President of Peking University [and Christian by faith], at Harvard University in 1936, he said: "With the new aids of modern science and technology, and of the new social and historical sciences, we are confident that we may yet achieve a rapid liberation from the two thousand years of cultural domination (by India)."

The decline of Buddhism began much earlier and was concomitant consequence of the decline in India, as also due to the rise of Confucius ethic and Tao School in China. This decline led to a weakening of contacts between China and India, after the tenth century. Over next two centuries, trade and commerce between India and China also declined on account of a number of political developments such as Islamic invasions, and, gradually, thus whatever little residual contacts existed began to fade with the advent of the colonial and imperialist era in Asia.

Considering that modern China had emerged out of a communist revolution, now as a proud globally influential power, it should surprise no one that China soon wished to underplay her past 'Sanskritization', even to seek to make it to be a non-topic.

## III

In order to understand the extent of past Sanskritization of China, we need to be clear about two things: First, it was Mahayana Buddhism that went to China, and the basic doctrines and principles of Mahayana were in Sanskrit, and not in Pali and conceptually very close to Hinduism. Second, the date of Buddha's *Nirvana* is not 483 B.C. as Western writers claim, and which date Indian historians are prone to recycle but much earlier, and judged by Tibetan records, probably as old as 2000 B.C..

It is curious that Indian historians seem completely oblivious of Fa Hsien's account on the subject. Fa Hsien's account was translated into French in 1836 by Abel-Remusat, into English by Beal (1869), Giles (1877, 1923), Legge (1886), and Li Yung Tin's (1957), the semi-official Chinese translation. All except the last are poor translations.

The most commonly used is James Legge (1886), but the translation contains as much of Legge as Fa Hsien's account. His footnotes are especially bad. The Li translation was made in Beijing in 1957, but suffers in being quite stylised, and reflects the modern Chinese desire to underplay the extent of Sanskritization of China.

For instance, the title of Fa Hsien's work is translated as: Fa Hsien's Record of the Buddhistic Countries. The original Chinese reads: An Account of the Sramana Fa-hsien of His Travels to India. 'Sramana' is a Sanskrit word meaning holy priest. The original account describes Fa Hsien as being distressed by the lack of understanding in China of Buddhist principles, and so decided to go to India to obtain documents to further the understanding of Mahayana Buddhism in China. The 1957 Li translation says "Fa Hsien was distressed to observe that not all the canons of the Monastic Rules was obtainable in China." For this reason, this translation says: "Fa Hsien and his friends went to India to obtain these rules and regulations." That is, Fa Hsien did not go to attain better spiritual understanding, but to obtain documents, just as one would go to a library. Such underplaying is understandable especially since even modern Indians find the Hu Shih's perception incredible.

Now, when did Buddhism first reach China? The Fa Hsien version records: "The monks asked Fa Hsien [after they had crossed the Indus] if he knew when the law of Buddha first travelled to the East." Fa Hsien replied: "I asked the various people [of those eastern countries] and they all agree that it was introduced long ago. After Maitreya [Bodhisatva] image was set up by them, Indian sramanas (priestly class) continuously crossed this river bringing scriptures and disciplines. The image was set up about 300 years after Buddha attained Nirvana, during the time of King Ping of the Chou Dynasty. So we may say that the spread of the Great Religion dates from the time of that image."

From this statement of Fa Hsien we may derive two historical statements of fundamental importance: First, Buddha attained Nirvana about 300 hundred years prior to reign of King Ping of the Chou Dynasty. Even by Western chronology of Chinese historical events, King Ping's reign was between 770 B.0 to 720 B.C. Taking therefore 750 B.C. as the date of Maitreya's image, this places Buddha's Nirvana at about 1050 B.C. However, Ping's reign could well be earlier. The dates in vogue today have been assigned by Western historians, and they could have got the chronology of Chinese history as wrong as that of Indian history.

Second, going by Fa Hsien's account, Buddhism entered China much before than we had thought earlier, i.e., sometime before 750 B.C.. There is thus much scope for further research here, especially in regard to the relation between Ashoka and the Chinese Kings. Also, we can now, on Fa Hsien's account, discount the theory that Confucius and Buddha were contemporaries.

It is also interesting to see how Western historians have reacted to Fa Hsien's account. For example, Max Muller who had got Indian chronology all wrong, wrote a review: "Buddhism and Buddhist Pilgrims" [in the (London) Times dated April 17 & 20, 1857] and in this review he placed Buddha's Nirvana at around 500 B.C..

What is surprising is that he makes almost no mention of Fa Hsien in this regard in his entire article. He was certainly aware of the translation of Abel-Remusat as he indicates towards the end of his article. Legge's version is on the other hand full of *nonsequitor:*

"As King Ping's reign lasted from B.C. 750 to 719, this would place the death of Buddha in the eleventh century B.C..... But if Rhys David be correct, as I think he is, in fixing the date of Buddha's departing within a few years of 412 B.C. .., then the Buddha was very considerably the junior Confucius." [*A Record of Buddhistic Kingdoms*, Clarendon Press, Oxford (1886), p. 28].

During the last 50 years Western writers on Sino-Indian

history have developed the following view on Fa Hsien, perhaps to discredit him: First, they hold that Fa Hsien may have been a devout monk, but that his historical sense was poor. To support this, they point out that Fa Hsien does not even once mention Vikramaditya, or Chandragupta. Given that Vikramaditya represents the peak of Hindu revival during whose time Fa Hsien was reportedly in India, should he not have mentioned him even once? There is a rebuttal for this. Second, they say, when Fa Hsien says it was 300 years after Buddha's Nirvana that Maitreya's image was built, it does not mean much. Since Fa Hsien is very vague on other matters. It could just as well be just 3 years!

These arguments do not hold water, because Fa Hsien's account is full of accurate description of topography, the hospitality of the people etc. It is true that he made not a single mention of Chandragupta, but that is easy to understand because Chandragupta, to put it simply, did not live then. His reign was around 300 B.C..

Western historians have determined Chandragupta's reign in AD circa 400, on the arbitrary assumption that "Sandrocottos" of Megasthenes is Chandragupta Maurya. But this arbitrary determination of Western historians is under challenge today. In my view, the Western view is wrong, and that Megasthenes' Sandrocottos was instead Gupta Chandragupta, not Maurya.

The second argument also leaves much to be desired. It merely points out that these people have not read Fa Hsien. He is quite precise as the following passage in his narration shows:

"While in this world, he (Buddha) spent 45 years expounding the Law, teaching and edifying the people, those without peace he gave peace, those without salvation he gave salvation. When he fulfilled his mission, he attained Nirvana. Since his Nirvana, 1497 years ago, the Eye of the World has been closed and all the living creatures have never ceased to grieve."

There is no doubt that the Sino-Indian contact has been at least more than 3000 years, mostly friendly, and for a long period culturally unidirectional from India to China. In 1949, we should have charted a course of mutually beneficial relations based on these forty centuries old contacts, and not allowed the relatively more recently formed nations such as the USA and the now defunct USSR to mould it to serve their own strategic interests of and to disrupt this historic Asian compact. Together, China and India constitute even today 36 per cent of the world's population.

It would thus be appropriate to first understand the sequence and depth of Sino-Indian relations in the historical perspective. Few scholars have attempted that. For all his other faults, K.M. Panikkar is the only one I know of, who comprehended the reality of the hoary Sino-Indian history, even if had he fumbled on the Communist Chinese intentions on Tibet and Sino-Indian border. I have here relied on his seminal works in the field.

## IV

At the centre of the Gobi Desert, an oasis known as Yumen, (i.e., 'Jade Gate'] which is on the border of former Chinese Empire, houses a valley sheltered by hills on all sides, known now the world over as Dunghuan. There, on the sides of the hills, are excavated hundreds of caves, beautified by mural paintings and sculptures of 'very high quality, depicting scenes from the life of Buddha and from the Jataka stories. The Dunghuan caves, represented a great international monastery.

Dunghuan was the last stage of the journey from India and the Indianised kingdoms of Central Asia to the great empire of China. It was the last resting place, before entering China proper, of the scholars, missionaries and other travellers who were continuously arriving from India, and other areas of the Buddhist civilisation, as also the first stage for those undertaking the strenuous journey across the snows of the Pamirs, or the desert lands of Central Asia, to visit the holy places of Buddhism in India. At Dunghuan, the three northern routes from India met. It was the great clearing-house for all travellers to China from the north-west, and the monastery with its temples, caves for mediation and large collection of books provided an ideal resting place.

Of the three routes, the first lay through Afghanistan, with stages at Jalalabad, then known as Nagarahara, and at Bamiyan. French archaeologists have shown us what a great centre of Indian culture Bamiyan was in the first millennium of the Christian Era. From there, through Bactria, the area of Samarkand, the route went eastwards over the passes of the Tien Shan Mountains. A second route which was shorter but more difficult lay through Kashmir and Gilgit to Kashgar, and from there to Tokhau. A third was directly to Kashgar and from there along the Tarim basin to Dunghuan.

All along these route there flourished kingdoms, great and small, the population of which professed Buddhism, spoke Sanskrit and had accepted Indian culture, till Islamic forays destroyed it all, and laid it to ruins. A large number of manuscripts have now been discovered in this region and most of them are in Indian script of the Kushan and Gupta periods.

Some of the dynasties, which ruled in these areas, were also of Indian origin. In fact, up to the very borders of China on its north-west side, kingdoms which had imbibed the spirit of Indian culture were in existence at least from the first century A.D. till the emergence of the Ching dynasty in China, and the onslaught of Islam in India.

Thus India, China and Iran were the pivots on which turned the cultural dynamics of most of Asia. The route across Tibet, it should be noted developed at a later period and was never important from a commercial point of view. But it however endured.

Another important route to China was by sea. The maritime routes to the Pacific Ocean were known to the coastal peoples of India from the earliest periods of history. As during the first century of the Christian Era we have allusions in Chinese records to the existence of Hinduised kingdoms in who was known as Indo-China, where the Chinese had also penetrated, the two civilisations may be said to have confronted and fused with each other there at least from that time.

There was a continuous intercourse between the ports of India and these Hinduised states and also directly between the Indian ports and south China [25). There were thus three main lines of communication between India and China in past history: Across Central Asia by many different routes, via Bamiyan and Bactriana; via Kashgar across the Tarim Valley; and via Kashmir, Gilgit and Yasin across the Pamirs.

These routes became important alter the 2nd century B.C., and till the middle of the 9th century A.D., when Islam interposed an effective barrier, they continued to be the most important highways of communication. The earliest route via

Assam and Burma never fell into actual disuse, though it lost much of its importance for India as a whole after the growth of traffic across Central Asia. Then the sea communications grew continuously in importance, especially for South India and, till the blockade of the Chinese coast by the Portuguese, were of the highest importance to Sino-Indian relations. In South Indian literature of the 13th and 14th centuries, junks and sampans are frequently mentioned. From Quilon in Kerala on the west coast, ships sailed regularly to the ports of South China and it is in one of these that Archbishop Montecorvino travelled to the Far East. The last visit of Cheng Ho's armada to the port of South India was in 1424 A.D.

## V

When did India first come into contact with its great neighbour? European scholars were of the view that the first contact was not before the establishment of the Chin Dynasty by Shih Huang Ti (the first emperor) in 221 B.C. But by Fa Hsien's account, we now know that this is not well founded. Though, at present no specific date can be given for the discovery of China by India, it is probably true that India was in contact with the south-western regions of China from the earliest period of history. After the establishment of the Chin Empire and the unification of China, the intercourse became much deeper and closer, when between the north-west of China and the Gandhara region, the Kushans and a number of 'Indianised' kingdoms developed relations fully that held for over a thousand years.

Dr. Hu Shih had however told the then Indian Ambassador K.M. Panikkar that the earliest contacts of Buddhism with

China were through the southern route. Later, no doubt, with the more extensive relations established through the Indo-Buddhist kingdoms of Central Asia, the southern influence seems to have become less important, but obviously that it did not at any time cease because or the existence in Szechuan of Sanskrit inscriptions and the continuing influence of Tantric worship in south-western China.

Because of the sea route, the trade with South India developed separately. Diplomatic relations were also established between the South Indian courts and the Chinese Empire. According to Panikkar, a Chinese writer, Pan Kou, who lived at the end of the 1st century, mentioned that in the time of Han emperor, the Chola kings sent emissaries to China. The route given by Pan Kou as well as the name of state indicates that the kingdom ought to be of Cholas in Kanchi. It is also stated that Wang Ming, the ruler in 1st century A.D., sent presents to the Kanchi king. Pan Kou adds that the exports from South India were 'shining pearls, rare gems, and strange products' which the Chinese received in exchange for silk and gold. Pan Kou also makes it clear that these were brought to China on Indian ships.

As Panikkar points out, the territories of Sri Vijaya included both the Malay Peninsula and Sumatra and, in the day of its glory, also a major portion of Java. For over seven hundred years this Chola state in Hindu tradition, controlled communications between the Indian Ocean and the Pacific and was the intermediary in the cultural and commercial traffic between India and China.

With the arrival of the Portuguese in 1450 A.D. the sea route was closed to Chinese vessels. Over the next four centuries, India's connection with China were through the

Europeans. In the early 19th century Indian merchants re-appeared in China, but under the British flag. The great Parsi houses of Bombay,, especially the Camas, and Chinoys participated in Chinese trade. Small Indian trading communities came to be established at Canton, Shanghai and Tientsin and other treaty ports. They were but merely subsidiary to British trade and could not however be said to have materially contributed to the relations between China and India.

Paradoxically today, as Panikkar regretfully notes, every schoolboy in India knows the names of Fa Hsien, Yuan Chuan and I-Tsing, but does not know anything of the great number of very distinguished Indian scholars who spent their lives in China, translating Indian books, teaching in monasteries and generally propagating Indian thought.

The earliest known Indian scholar to reach China was Kashyapa Matanga, who was in China in A.D. 65. Kashyapa Matanga with Dharma Ratna who had reached Loyang, had come from today's Madhya Pradesh.

One of the best remembered and most notable Indian scholar was Kumarajiva (end of 4th century). Between the time of Kashyapa Matanga and Kumarajiva, Indian culture had penetrated into China both from the North and from the south of India.

Kumarajiva, the son of an Indian scholar from Kashmir. Kumarayana who had established himself in Kouchi as a great scholar, was born around A.D. 343. His mother, formerly a Buddhist nun, encouraged him in his career as a Buddhist priest. At age 9, she entrusted his schooling to Bandhu Datta, who was a celebrated sarvastivadin and from him Kumarajiva had his first training in Buddhist doctrines.

Three years later, when he was only 12, he met Buddha Yasas at Kashgar and was converted to the Mahayana doctrine. Kumarajiva was a student of the Vedas as well [see: Libenthal, W.: *The Book of Chao* (p. 67)]. He had therefore mastered both Hindu and Buddhist learning.

After completing his studies, Kumarajiva returned to Kuchi, and achieved an international reputation as a scholar, teacher and expounder of Buddhist doctrines. The Chin Emperor was so impressed by the fame of Kumarajiva that he sent an envoy, to ask the Kuchi king to send Kumarajiva to the Imperial Court.

But Kumarajiva was reluctant to go, and therefore the King did not assent. This was resented by the Chinese envoy who declared war on the king and, after defeating him in A.D. 385, kidnapped the monk to China! In the meantime, the Emperor of China had been murdered, and therefore the envoy who had kidnapped Kumarajiva, kept the monk with himself. In 401, when he was nearly 60 years old Kumarajiva reached Chang An, the imperial capital of the new Emperor of China.

Kumarajiva was from childhood at home in Sanskrit. In Kuchi, where he was born, he had already become familiar with Chinese and he had now an opportunity of correcting the imperfections of the provincial dialect during his sixteen years stay in Gansu as the guest of the general. When he arrived at the Imperial Court, he had become equally at home in classical Sanskrit and in Chinese, and therefore an ideal interpreter of Indian culture to China. The Emperor You Chang accorded him unusual honours and made the *Raj Guru* (or Guo Shih).

For the next twelve years, till his death in 413, Kumarajiva was engaged in translating Buddhist texts and correcting earlier translations. A Bureau of Translators was set up under

Kumarajiva's supervision, with over eight hundred scholars on the staff. Over 106 works, including most of the Mahayana texts, were translated. Of these, fifty-six are still available, and waiting for scholars to delve into.

By then Kumarajiva who had begun as a follower of Hinayana, had become a staunch Mahayanist. Till Kumarajiva's time, Chinese Buddhism seems to have been mainly of the Hinayana school. It is Kumarajiva's apostolate in China that established Mahayana as the dominant school of Chinese Buddhism and, consequently, that was responsible for the spread of that school in the Far East. From that point of view alone, Kumarajiva's contribution could well be said to be of the highest historical significance.

A revolutionary teacher who is still revered in China is Bodhi Dharma, who belonged to a royal family of Kanchipuram in South India. Bodhi Dharma preached the doctrine that the only reality is the Buddha nature in the heart of man, and the realisation of that Buddha-nature can only come from direct experience and not by learning or asceticism. This represented the first introduction of Hindu mysticism in Buddhist garb into China.

Bodhi Dharma lived in the Shao Lin Monastery, and meditated in silence for nine years. There he invented 'Wu Shih', the martial arts of self-defence that Japan later imported. Modern India even today does not know that ancient India gave Karate to the world.

Vajrabodhi a priest from Kerala, introduced the Mantra Sastra into China. He had attained sufficient eminence in sciences to become the guru of the King of Kanchi. Late in life he converted to Tantric Buddhism. After some years at Nalanda, he, with his chief disciple, Amogha Vajra, left for China for sea, reaching there in 719 in his 58th year.

The Mantra sect which Vajrabodhi established was tantric esoterism, based on mulct mantras, and on worship of Devi through Yantras or diagrams as practised among the Saktas in India. Its Buddhist counterpart is generally in the Vajra Yana form.

Thus, it was not only Buddhism that had penetrated into China. Sankhya, tantra sastras, and other Hindu beliefs were also introduced into the thought of that country. How much of the Hinduism was included in this vast export of ideas may be seen from the fact that in the vast collection which Dr. Raghuvira brought back from China, there is a third century summary of the Ramayana story.

Another source of Sanskritization was through Tibet. In the middle of the 6th century, Srong Tsang unified the clans of Tibet. His son, Srong Tsand Gampo, introduced into Tibet a modified Indian alphabet based on Nagari. It was King Srong Be Tsan (740-786) who invited numerous Indian scholars to Tibet, notably Shanta Rakshita (747 AD), who became his guru. It was at his suggestion that the great Padma Sambhava, known as Guru Rimpoche, the precious teacher, was invited to Tibet. Padma Sambhava was the founder of the Tantric sect of Buddhism in Tibet.

Tibet became the land of great monas-teries under his inspiration, and Tibetan tantricism secured a great hold on the border nationalities of China. In the Yuan on Mongolian period, Lamaism became a fashion as the emperor himself accepted the creed. The Tibetan monk, Phago-pa, was invited to the Mongol court in 1256, by Kublai Khan. Kublai made him Raj Guru [Scholar Laureate of the State] and recognised him as the head of the Buddhist 'Church'. It is he who invented the alphabetic system for the Mongol language.

This position of influence continued even under the Manchus i.e., the Ching Dynasty. The Buddhism that reached China, Mongolia and other countries through Tibet was of the Tantric variety. Further, it led to a penetration of especially the Saivite cults into China, a subject which has so far not been studied at all. In the collection brought back by Dr. Raghuvira, there is a banner with the Gayatri mantra written on it in Mongolian characters.

The Buddhist religion however did not reach China as a system of elaborate metaphysics and spiritual discipline as Panikkar has astutely noted, but as a form of popular worship and belief gradually taking root among the people, probably the poorest and the most lowly to whom the Buddhist missionaries, traders and travellers had brought the good tidings of mercy and delivery from pain.

The apparently rapid progress made by Buddhism in the Yangtze Valley and on the southern coast towards the end of the second century seems to indicate that it had a long period of slow but steady permeation among the people. By the third century, when the men of letters began to admire and defend it, Buddhism had already become a powerful religion, not because there was governmental patronage of which there was but very little, but because of its powerful following among the people.

It was the common man's religion and it continued to be so. Equally significant is that, the number of Chinese pilgrims and scholars who visited India was unusually large. Of these the names of Fa Hsien, Yuan Chuan (Hiouen Tsang), and I-tsing are well known. But the general idea that with the downfall of the Tang dynasty Chinese pilgrims ceased to frequent holy places in India or pursue their studies at Indian centres of learning is false. That this was not so is amply proved by the Chinese inscriptions discovered at Bodh Gaya. In the Revue de L'histoire des Religions (1896), the famous scholar Cliavannes has analysed these inscriptions, and concluded:

"The Chinese pilgrims who went to India in this period (in the 10th and 11th centuries] were numerous...."

## VI

No wonder, because of the dominance of Indian thought in China for a period of over six hundred years and the continuance of Buddhism in its naturalised form as one of the principal factors in Chinese life even now, the great Chinese philosopher, Dr Hu Shill, in his 1936 Harvard discourse titled "The Indianisation of China" had concluded that: "The long history of Indianisation of Chinese institutions, thought, art, and life in general furnishes the most extensive material that can be found for the study of cultural borrowings on the grandest scale."

Dr. Hu Shih's description of the acceptance of Buddhisin by the masses of China in the 4th, 5th and 6th centuries is worth quoting:

"Then there came the great religion of the Buddha together with all the Mahayana trimmings of the pre-Buddhist and non-Buddhist religions of India. Never before had China seen a religion so rich in imagery, so beautiful and captivating in ritualism and so bold in cosmological and metaphysical speculations. Like a poor beggar suddenly halting before magnificent storehouse of precious stones of dazzling brilliancy and splendour, China was overwhelmed, baffled and overjoyed. She begged and borrowed freely from the munificent giver. The first borrowings were chiefly from the religious life of India, in which China's indebtedness to India can never be fully told. India gave China, for example, not only one paradise but tens of paradises; not only Hell but many hells, each varying in severity and horror from the other. The old simple idea of retribution of good and evil was replaced by the idea of the transmigration of the soul and the iron law of Karma which runs through all past, present and future existences. These and thousands of other items of belief and practice have poured from India by land and by sea into China and have been accepted and gradually made into parts of the cultural life of China."

Naturally, with such a people as the Chinese, justly proud of their own long-established civilisation, with their distinctive attitude towards life, with their own philosophies, this wholesale acceptance of what was essentially a foreign religion, with its attendant culture, could not proceed for long without strenuous opposition.

Such opposition soon developed from the Confucian literati who not only defended Confucianism vigorously but counter-attacked Buddhist doctrines, especially the tendency of converts to become monks and to renounce their families and to practise celibacy—both directly opposed to the strong familial tradition of Chinese civilisation and its emphasis on both ancestor-worship and on posterity. As a result of this organised counter-attack, Indian influence in China had to face four periods of serious and sustained persecution, in A.D. 446, 574, 845 and 955. As Dr. Hu Shih states: "It is significant to note that all edicts for the persecution of Buddhism emphasised the fact that it was an alien religion and that it was a national disaster and a humiliation for the Celestial Empire to be thus under the influence of aliens."

But these exhibitions of imperial power and nationalist reaction had never more than temporary success. Indian influence had gone too deep, and had penetrated the masses to such an extent that, whatever the official policy or the orders issued, the Sanskritization movement went on apace.

After the 10th century, however, the religious fervour for Buddhism began to decline. Dr. Hu Shih explained this as being due to the twin process of domestication and assimilation. "Look at the faces of the deities in a Buddhist temple in China today," he stated, "and trace each to its earliest Indian original and you will realise how this process of domestication has worked ... Maitreya, for example, has now become the big-bellied, heartily laughing Chinese monk that greets you as you enter any Buddhist monastery in China. Indeed, all faces of the Buddhist deities have been Sinicised through a long but unconscious process of domestication."

Indian influence on Chinese sculpture and painting is well known and does not require to be restated here. In regard to drama, scholars trace three stages: first when the technique and the story and the characters were borrowed from India. Slowly, while the story and the characters remained Indian, the technique was suitably altered to meet Chinese requirements. In the third stage, the Chinese characters replace the Indian and the story is suitably modified. A new national Chinese drama came into being in which Indian influences can only be noticed by scholars.

Even in music the following quotation from Chinese Literature [4th issue 1955, p. 164], an official publication of the People's Republic, explains the position:

"As early as the Sui dynasty (A.D. 581-618), Indian music was formally recognized by the Chinese government as one of the chief categories of music. Later, during the Tang dynasty (A.D. 615-907) the tune of a Brahmin Dance which as introduced into China from the North West, became, after a certain amount of modification, the melody of the celebrated Rainbow Garment Dance. This melody was so popular with the Chinese of the Tang dynasty that the famous poet, Pai Chu Yi wrote a poem in praise of it. It is little wonder that when a Chinese audience today hears Indian music they feel that while possessing a piquant India flavour it has a remarkable affinity with Chinese music."

The final conclusions of Dr. Hu Shih are worth quoting:

"What had happened during these thousand years to bring about such a tremendous difference in the Chinese outlook on life? Nothing but the gradual deepening and intensifying of the Indianisation of Chinese thought, life and institutions. Buddhism was fading away, but its cultural content had been domesticated and appropriated by the secular thinkers and had penetrated into Chinese life and institutions far beyond the confines of the monasteries and nunneries of Buddhism ... in these and many other aspects the great philosophers of esoteric rationalism [in China] were unconsciously acting as the most effective agents for the final Indianisation of China."

Was Sino-Indian relations during the first millennium of the 'Christian Era', a one-way traffic, in which India gave and China received, leading so distinguished and objective a scholar as Hu Shih to describe the movement as the "Indianisation of China"? Scholars however recognize that such one-sided influence even if unidirectional has an implicit bilateral content. The bilateral contacts were so vigorous and extended over such a long period that it would be absurd to deny the influence of Chinese civilization on India.

The wide prevalence of silk from very earliest times is attested to by literature. Fruits of different kinds, especially pears and peaches as noted by Yuan Chuan were intro-duced from China, as also the lichi which still retains its Chinese name. Vermilion probably came first from China. In the south of India, the technique of the fishing industry in the backwaters seems to have been introduced from Canton. Also, it is well known that a flourishing porcelain industry was introduced into Kerala by the Chinese. In fact, it is known that a small colony of Chinese existed near Quilon for many centuries.

The architecture in Kerala of houses is distinctly Chinese. (or is the causation vice versa?) Intimate religious, cultural and social relations existed between. the two major civilizations of Asia for a period of nearly fifteen hundred years. For nearly a thousand years, from the first century B.C. to the 10th century A.D., it was one of the major facts of the world's cultural history. Its importance in shaping the mind of East Asia, including Japan, Korea and Mongolia, is something which cannot be overlooked. The Asian mind as of a community of ideas, beliefs and traditions is the contribution of this close association of the Indian and Chinese peoples over so long a period.

That two giant ancient civilizations with so much past interaction and cultural borrowing should have quarrelled in the twentieth century AD—as something that happened never before in history—is a pathetic commentary on the myopic vision and quality of leadership on both sides of the Himalayas, however asymmetric or uneven may be the burden of responsibility placed for that folly.

Time has thus come for Indian foreign policy to be redesigned and restructured on a comprehensive substantive basis, consistent now with India's growing economic power and past history, to maximize the geostrategic advantage by transparent initiatives and by exercising fresh options that fosters our national security.

By national security, I mean peace on our borders, control of internal insurgency, and mutually beneficial understanding with key countries of the world. All three components are interconnected. The Naga-Mizo-Manipur problem, for example, became easier to man-age during the 1978-84 period because of the initiatives, mostly mine, taken then to improve relations with China. It is an immutable fact today that the internal insurgency problems in Kashmir will become easier to manage when we ensure peace on the Pakistan border. Pakistan may deny that it fosters insurgencies, but it is undeniable that hostility with countries makes it possible for the insurgents to have safe supply routes, and find easy places for rest and recuperation. Here too, China is relevant.

It is the central theme of this chapter that the fulcrum in redesigning of our foreign policy is the Sino-Indian relation. The strategic importance of engaging China in a constructive, if not cooperative, relationship has however not dawned on Indian leaders in government for a number of reasons, most of it due to miscalculations and misconceptions. Time is now to cut through these cobwebs and see the importance for India of China, with clarity, and in correct perspective.

The question before the nation is not whether India can dare to annoy China or not. The crucial query instead is: what should be its policy towards China: friendship or adversorial? Since 1978 when the Janata Party Government initiated the normalization, there has emerged a growing and now an overwhelming consensus in the country that we should befriend China, irrespective of what had happened in the past.

More important, there are sound strategic reasons for that consensus: First, it is the unanimous opinion of India's Defence Chiefs that defending against a China-Pakistan joint attack is nearly impossible for her armed forces at the present level of equipment and manpower, a reality that shall remain so for the foreseeable future. Therefore, India should strive for its security's sake, to separate China and Pakistan however onerous and difficult the task may be. Second, China is geo-strategically located to cause India if China wants to, enormous problems in Kashmir, UP border, Sikkim and Assam. Furthermore, in combination with Pakistan such problems will have a multiplier effect.

Mrs Indira Gandhi had understood this strategic fact even if late, especially in the context of the 1980-84 AASU agitation in Assam. I was in fact specifically requested by Mrs Gandhi in 1981 to discover the Chinese intention on this agitation, by raising it with Chairman Deng Xiao ping whom she knew I was to meet as scheduled to appreciate my contribution to the thawing of relation since 1977 when the Janata Party came to power at the Centre. [see Appendix III.] And now it is an established truth that since 1981, China consistently discouraged any attempt by extremist Assam agitators to go to China illegally across the borders to internationalize the issue. India thus gained tremendously by this cooperative non-interference by China.

Leaving aside for the moment the other possible positive gains from India-China friendship such as in the UN, in bilateral trade etc., these two immutable strategic facts make it imperative that any Indian government strive for Sino-Indian rapprochement. This basic strategic understanding and sense of history unfortunately has eluded comprehension of China-baiters in India, most of whom unfortunately are in office today in government.

The bare fact is that Sino-Indian relations today are not warm and cooperative, even if it is normalized and interactive. The question is why not? Is it rivalry, the border dispute, or something else?

In my view, China would not regard the border dispute as an obstacle to a warm strategic partnership with India. China has borders with 14 nations, and except India, it has resolved its disputes with all others including Russia. India has borders with six countries, and except Bhutan, we have disputes with all five others. Therefore on the question of border dispute, it is India which has much to be defensive about, not China.

Nor is rivalry the reason, since there are hardly any international issues in which India and China have irresolvable fundamental conflicts of interest. Nor, as we have seen in Chapter 1, over thousands of years of contact, there is a history of hostility between the two countries. Therefore, it is that 'something else' that irritates and disrupts our relations with China from time to time. That something else is India's Hindu ambivalence and lack of transparency in dealings with China on Tibet. In China's case, it's 'middle kingdom' pride in not bluntly articulating with India its concerns on Tibet.

It is essential in India's strategic interest to befriend China, and pay the price for it. That means, according to my understanding of the situation, squarely resolving the contradictions between our legitimate concerns in Tibet with our commitment enshrined in a 1954 treaty to recognize

Chinese sovereignty over Tibet. If the latter i.e., our commitment, is made transparent, consistent and demonstrable, the main hurdle in our relations with China will go. Then expressing our concerns to China on Tibet in bilateral meetings would not only not be misunderstood, but China would be obliged to willingly accommodate these concerns as well.

For this to transpire, India must re-orient its policy and the Indian mind purged of the inherited British duplicity on Tibet: which was to keep Tibetan status nebulous in everyone's mind by concocting a feudal concept of "suzerainty." This made Tibet as neither independent nor a part of China, i.e., in a trishanku state. This purging of the imperialist perfidy is the responsibility of the Indian Government. It cannot be done by any other institution in our society.

However, the present Government has been hamstrung by the pro-independent Tibet and Taiwan lobbies within the government. As recent as December 17, 1998, India's then Defence Minister George Fernandes, penned a Fore-word for a Penguin edition of deceased journalist D.R. Mankekar's book: The Guilty Men of 1962. In that, Fernandes to promote his commitment to the anti-Chinese pro-Tibet independence lobby, called the book, a "masterpiece," and added: "The well-fostered myth that the danger to India's security threat comes from Pakistan has now been exploded, and a new realism of India's threat perception has begun to take root in its place." That new 'realism' of course, was to perceive China as a danger to India. But recent events expose the vapidity of that perception.

The Dalai Lama's entourage has invested his Holiness' treasure chest of gold and jewels in the USA, and in property deals in India. The Dalai Lama's advisers have supported certain Indian politicians, at the time of elections. The Dalai Lama has also permitted Tibetan doctors to prescribe herbal treatment for a top BJP leader. These politicians today therefore privately obliged, are hell bent on disrupting Sino-Indian relations, and in not allowing it to develop to the point where the locus standi of the Dalai Lama presence in India could become untenable.

The crux of my thesis thus is that Sino-Indian relations can never become close, friendly and a warm partnership unless our blind spot on Tibet is removed, and China is reassured. I advocate therefore that we have to digest and internalize the view that the shortest political route to Lhasa is via Beijing, and not across the Himalayas. Dalai Lama, therefore, is welcome to stay in India as a spiritual leader, but not as a head of an 'exile' government.

If the Dalai Lama advisers get derailed by fawning Hollywood actors, then it is better that the Dalai Lama is advised to do his politics stationed in Beverley Hills, California and not from Indian soil. India has no special responsibility to host the Dalai Lama. In the entire 2000 years of Sino-Indian history can the Bureau of the Dalai Lama give a single example when Tibet stood up for India? Lhasa had even laid claims to Tawang when India was weak, and Tibet was temporarily an independent country, e.g., in 1946.

The status of Tibet, and our perception of it, has been one of the destabilising factors in Sino-Indian relations. Publicly, the Indian government regards Tibet as an integral part of China. But in popular parlance, and in many of our actions, we do not behave as if Tibet is a part of China. For example, the Indian government had raised in the 1980s a highly paid special service unit, a 8000-strong commando group of Tibetans, who woke up every morning in the special camps with cries of "Long live Dalai Lama. We shall liberate Tibet."

This commando group is still under the active supervision of the Research and Analysis Wing (RAW) and the Cabinet Secretariat. If we regard Tibet as part of China, then why is there need for maintaining such a special group? Why not instead a regular army unit with contingency plans? The Indian government has never answered this query of mine.

The treatment extended to the Dalai Lama also reveals this ambivalence in our attitude towards Tibet. The government says that India has only extended political asylum to the Dalai Lama, because otherwise his life would be in danger if he returns to Tibet. But the Bureau of the Dalai Lama is quite active in New Delhi propagating the thesis that Tibet is an independent country. If the Indian government sincerely believed that Tibet is a part of China, then the activities of the Bureau of the Dalai Lama should be considered as no less repugnant than the activities of the Khalistan "government" and of Jagjit Singh Chaultan in the United Kingdom.

If our intentions on the Tibetan question are honourable, then it is necessary for transparent diplomacy that these intentions be understood as such. Alternatively, if we believe Tibet to be an independent country, and want to liberate it, then an entirely different course in our diplomacy and military strategy is called for. Today, we are getting the worst of both positions. We accept Tibet as a part of China, and yet we allow the seeds of doubt to germinate in the mind of our giant neighbour about our intentions. Sino-Indian relations thus suffer.

Two basic questions need to be answered if we have to have a clear cut Tibet policy: First, was Tibet an independent country at any point in history? Second, can Tibet be a viable independent country at some point in the not-very-distant future? While the first question belongs to the realm of historical research, it is the second question which we have to answer before forming our national security policy. In this chapter, I shall seek to answer both questions.

The latter question, however, was asked and answered in 1950 by the then Congress government, and again the same question was asked and answered by the Janata Party government in 1977-78. On both occasions, the two governments of the Congress and the united Janata Party respectively, found the answer in the negative: Tibet could not be sustained as an independent country.

In the period 1977-78, the Janata government also reconsidered the question of Tibet in the light of the support given to Tibetan independence by two then Janata minis-ters, Raj Narain and George Fernandes. But as Foreign Minister A.B. Vajpayee (who earlier used to vociferously support Tibetan independence) stated in the Lok Sabha while answering Lok Sabha Starred Question No. 247 on March 8, 1979 on behalf of the Morarji Desai led Janata Party government, the following: "We regard Tibet as a region of China. We would be happy if the Dalai Lama and the Tibetans go back (to Tibet) if they think that conditions are suitable to them."

In other words, the Janata Party government had concluded that Tibet is to be regarded as a part of China, and the implicit endeavour is that conditions become ripe so that the Dalai Lama himself feels that it is safe to return to Lhasa. New Delhi would neither ask the Dalai Lama to leave, nor ask him to stay: The decision was that of the Dalai Lama.

While the Indian government position has been categoric in nature, with no room for a second interpretation, there is nevertheless enough indication that Indian politicians in private have taken a stand inconsistent with stated government declaration.

For example, George Fernandes as the Janata government's minister-in-waiting for the USSR's Prime Minister Kosygin, in 1979 just four days after the Foreign Minister's reiteration on the floor of Parliament, argued with the visiting Soviet leader that the USSR should declare its support for independent Tibet. This plea of Fernandes was in complete violation of the Janata government commitment in Parliament, and thus reflected more the status of Fernandes as a captive of the Free Tibet lobby rather than a member of the Cabinet.

Excerpted below is the RAW transcript (that I got from Prime Minister Morarji Desai's memoirs that I had been asked to write) of the conversation between George Fernandes, Minister-in-Waiting and Alexei Kusygin, Soviet Premier, on route from Delhi to Baroda-Anand-Bangalore-Delhi, March 11-13, 1979. On 12.3.1979 while travelling from Anand to Baroda by car, the following exchange took place (interpreter's notes):

(*George Fernandes*) GF: Will you be prepared to take a stand to recognising independence of Tibet. The past Governments (of India) made a mistake in not doing so.

(*Alexei Kosygin*) K: I did not know that. Mrs Indira Gandhi when she came to Moscow told us that India was opposed to China's seizure of Tibet, regarded it as illegal, and that is why her Government was giving refuge to Dalai Lama. It is your (Janata) Government which supports the Chinese position. I heard it for the first time from your Foreign Minister (Vajpayee) two days ago.

GF: I and other like-minded persons always supported Tibet's right to freedom, and always criticized the Indian Government's failure to do so. The Janata Government should undo what the previous Governments had done.

K: It is question for the Indian Government. Soviet Government never suggested even in the fifties that China might conquer Tibet.

GE: Don't you think then a fresh statement is necessary about Tibet's Independence? From a mighty power like the USSR it would be a great encouragement.

K: Tibet is far from the Soviet Union and Soviet Union regards Tibet in India's exclusive sphere of influence. It is for India to take a stand. Anyway is there much of Tibet left? They have massacred them and forcibly married them.

GE: I draw great inspiration from your statement Lovers of Tibet freedom could count on Soviet Government's support if and when India takes a firm stand.

K: You are right.

The discussion between Kosygin and Fernandes also shows that when Mrs. Gandhi had privately told the Russians one thing, and the Indian Parliament another thing (namely that Tibet is a part of China).

In March 1983, while speaking on the foreign affairs debate, I had pointedly asked the following question: Does the government of India regard Tibet as a part of China or not? The then Foreign Minister, Narasimha Rao, on 31 March 1983, in reply, stated that the Congress(I) government did indeed regard Tibet as a part of China.

This declaration however did not square with other developments. In March 1983, 70 Congress(I) MPs signed a memorandum and sent it to the Prime Minister, Mrs Indira

Gandhi, asking her to give a Tibetan rebel delegation "observer" status in the Non-Aligned Conference. Could Congress(I) MPs have cared to sign such a memorandum without some guidance from above? Some Indians are sentimental about the status of Tibet vis-a-vis China. There is the undercurrent of unrealities which is responsible for this sentiment. But the national security consequence of such a sentiment If India promotes Tibetan independence, cannot China promote Kashmir, Assamese, Naga and Sikh secession?

And what does Tibetan history say? Have not Tibetan governments from 1890 to 1950 laid claim to Sikkim, Bhutan and the whole of Arunachal? Can India accept these consequential claims of an independent Tibet? The second question is that if India supports the independence of Tibet, can India sustain, it?

Today's Tibet province of China is only about a quarter of the ancient Tibet. This partition was formally recognized by Prime Minister Vajpayee when 2003 he went to Beijing to mollify the Chinese who were upset by the letter he had written in 1998 to US President Clinton blaming the threat from China for exploding hydrogen nuclear bombs that year.

The other areas have been amalgamated: Amdo in Qinghai Province, and Kham in Szechuan, Yunnan and Gansu. Even today's Tibet, which is more or less the—"outer Tibet" of British India's Foreign Secretary McMahon's, is 1.3 million square kilometres in area, one-third the size of India. It has a population of 2.0 million Tibetans. Can 1.3 million square kilometres of the most hazardous territory be defended by troops from India? *Note:* Well over half of Tibet's original territory has been appended to the contiguous Chinese provinces with only Central Tibet (U-Tsang) and parts of

Eastern Tibet (Kham) remaining as the so-called Tibet Autonomous Region.

The administrative incorporation into China of these vast areas serves to reduce the importance of Tibet, while also splitting the population, and accelerating their signification.

All population and other statistics regarding Tibet provided by official Chinese sources, refer only to the "Tibet Autonomous Region," and are consequently quite misleading.

Whereas the areas annexed to Western China are under provincial administration, the "Tibet Autonomous Region" is ruled by the Chinese Communist Party and the People's Liberation Army, through the Local Government of the "Autonomous Region." Recently a number of Tibetans have been appointed to high ranking but politically insignificant posts. All authority is actually vested in the hands of Chinese Party officials and military officers.

Even at the height of the 1959 Tibetan rebellion, the US State Department spokesman had merely stated. "The United States never regarded Tibet as an independent state." The USA has been, since 1979, in a strategic relationship with China. It never supported Tibetan independence before or after.

Russia at the height of its anti-China phobia (as USSR when Kosygin visited India in 1979), did not go beyond stating that Tibet was "in the exclusive sphere of India." Today, the residual Russia is busy negotiating with China almost like a junior partner. Russian President Vladimir Putin has even travelled to China to discuss an alliance with China.

In other words, it is only India, which seems left standing with the mantle of achieving Tibetan independence and sustaining it! And, why should India take on this responsibility? Once if Tibet becomes independent with Indian help, can India prevent the USA or the Russians from establishing a better rapport with Tibetans than India? Was India able to prevent Bangladesh from getting closer to the USA, China, or even rump Pakistan, and Saudi Arabia. These nations never even gave a thought it was the India's army which had liberated Bangladesh. Ironically all these countries had opposed the emergence of Bangladesh in the UN General Assembly.

Thus, it is wasteful and harmful for India's long term national interest to talk of Tibet's independence. As things stand, either Tibet has to be part of China or a part of India. India's option was lost by the foolish approach of Nehru who by his *nobless oblige* or plain Soviet subservience handed over Tibet to China on a platters without bargaining for acceptance of the 1912 Indo-Tibet agreement on the border, when Tibet was recognized independent nation. Nehru betrayed India's national interest in not obtaining a settlement on the border while negotiating the 1954 India- China Treaty on Tibet.

Nehru was also naive when he yielded to pressure in the late 1950s to train Khampas and Tibetans in Colorado in USA to regularly ambush Chinese military convoys inside Tibet. This sowed the seed of mistrust between China and India, leading to the sterile war of 1962. All this is not to suggest that the Chinese government is blameless in its handling of Tibetan affairs.

The Chinese army was allowed entry into Lhasa on 26 October 1951, after a 17-point agreement was signed between the Tibetan government in Lhasa and the government in Beijing. This was the culmination of events starting in January 1950 when the new Chinese government in Beijing sent a note to Tibet asking the Tibetans to "reunite with the motherland."

In October 1950, the Chinese army crossed Chinsha River from Szechuan province and liberated Chamdo, about 500 kilometres east of Lhasa. In April 1951, an authorised Tibetan delegation went to Beijing and on 23 May 1951 signed the 17-point agreement on the merger of Tibet with China. Thereafter, the Chinese army was welcomed to Lhasa with fervour and rejoicing. It is thus wrong to say that the Chinese army overran Tibet. Instead, the Chinese entered Lhasa to Tibetan welcome, as per the 17-point agreement.

Tibetans in India today denounce the 17-point agreement, and say it was done at the point of a gun. May be. But both the Dalai Lama and Panchen Lama during their visit to India in 1956 did not oppose this 17-point agreement. At that point, no gun was held to their head or probably Nehru advised them not to.

The Chinese government kept to the agreement till 1958. In that year under the Great Leap Forward programme launched by Chairman Mao the central government began to forcibly change the political and economic system in Tibet in the name of democratic reforms.

This was in violation of the 17-point agreement. In that agreement it was expressly stated (point 4) that "The central authorities will not alter the existing political system. The central authorities also will not alter the established status, functions and powers of the Dalai Lama. Officials of various ranks shall hold office as usual. "Similarly, point 11 expressly stated that there shall be no compulsion for carrying out reforms." Seeing these developments and fearing arrest and imprisonment, the Dalai Lama and nearly 100,000 Tibetans ran to safety in India, where they were given political asylum.

Later, during the period of the Cultural Revolution (1966-76), the 17-point agreement was torn to shreds by the Red Guards. Panchen Lama who had gone to Beijing in 1964, could not return to Lhasa till 1983 for this reason. Of the 1600 major monasteries, 1400 were destroyed.

In other words, from 1959 to 1977, the Chinese government had functioned in Tibet in breach of the 17-point agreement. In 1980, the Chinese Communist Party general secretary Hu Yaobang, and deputy Prime Minister, Wan Li, paid a visit to Tibet. That same year, the Chinese Communist Party issued new directives on Tibet, and Hu formally acknowledged "error and regret" for the trouble inflicted on the Tibetans during the earlier periods. The Chinese government officials also declared the need for preserving the "autonomy of Tibet," and new policies to that effect were announced.

On 15 December 1982, *Beijing Review,* the authoritative weekly magazine, published an editorial piece titled "Policy Towards the Dalai Lama." In it, it was said: "The Dalai Lama and his followers are welcome to return to China. Upon their return, the government will make appropriate political and personal arrangements for them."

The question thus remains whether today the conditions are ripe for the return of the Dalai Lama. If the Indian government is genuinely committed to its stated policy of regarding Tibet as a part of China, then it should be constantly in search of opportunities whereby the Dalai by himself feels that time has come when it is safe to go back to Lhasa.

Till the question of the Dalai Lama is satisfactorily resolved, the relations between India and China cannot be properly called normal. And the only satisfactory resolution of the Dalai Lama question is his safe return *and survival* in Tibet. But as a religious Buddhist divinity, Dalai Lama is always welcome in India. It is the clandestine exile government politics in Dharamshala that is endangering India's national interest.

Dalai Lama himself appears in two minds about his return. Sometime ago, he said in an interview in Far Eastern Economic Review: "During the past 20 years we have stood for independence not because we hated the Chinese or their ideology, but only because of the sufferings of our people. But circumstances change and we cannot hold on to the past."

Subsequently, he declared that he would visit Tibet. He has not done so far. It, however, seems that some Tibetan refugees in India are averse to the Dalai Lama even paying a visit to Lhasa.

While the veneration of the Dalai Lama inside Tibet even 25 years after his escape to India is amazing, refecting his ground level support amongst the Tibetans, it by no means can be taken for granted anymore. Even among monasteries in Tibet there are pro and anti-Dalai Lama factions.

During my June 2016 visit to Tibet, I found among the young generation, while they still respect the Dalai Lama, they reject the socio-economic order which existed earlier. The rest of Tibet seems in no mood for the kind of bloody revolt which would pave the way for the triumphant return of the Dalai Lama as the temporal head of independent Tibet.

Throughout history, the Chinese "suzerainty" over Tibet at least been an accepted fact even by governments hostile to China. But course of history has been uneven. There have been occasions when Tibet rebelled, but these have been for a short duration.

It was only on one occasion in 1913, when Dr. Sun Yat-Sen had toppled the Ch'ing dynasty monarchy in Beijing, that the 13th Dalai Lama (predecessor to the present Dalai Lama) declared Tibet as an independent country. But this was not for long. By 1929, Tibet under the same Dalai Lama, once again began to accept Chinese 'suzerainty' Incidentally, the Chinese always considered suzerainty to mean Chinese sovereignty with Tibetan autonomy, although in the Chinese Mandarin language a distinction is made indeed between sovereignty and suzerainty in assigning different characters.

It was Lord Curzon, the Imperial Viceroy of India who first raised the question of Tibet's independence. He regarded the idea of suzerainty as a "constitutional fiction." Curzon also directed Young husband to go to Lhasa (1903-04) to investigate if there was any Russian perfidy in Tibet. As a sequel to Young husband's expedition, an Anglo-Tibet.

Convention was signed in Lhasa in September 1904. The high points of this convention were that Tibet would deal directly with India instead of via China, and that Chumbi Valley will be given to India for 75 years. But Britain later handed back this vital valley to Tibet on a payment of a mere Rs. 2.5 million!

The British government in London rejected Curzon's moves, and ordered that an Anglo-Chinese convention be drafted to supersede the Anglo-Tibetan accord. This Curzon resisted by delaying tactics. Finally, London recalled Curzon, and sent Minto in his place. Later an Anglo-Chinese convention was signed on 27 April 1906 in Beijing, in which Chumbi Valley was returned to Tibet. Further vide Article 11 of the convention, the Chinese suzerainty over Tibet was reaffirmed.

To further confirm this, Britain and Russia signed the Anglo-Russian convention in St. Petersburg on 31 August

1907, in which Article 11 stated: "In conformity with the admitted principle of suzerainty of China over Tibet, Great Britain and Russia engage not to enter into negotiations with Tibet except through the intermediary of the Chinese government."

In other words, the British government reasserted its consistent stand formalised in 1890 when the first Anglo-Chinese convention was signed guaranteeing Chinese suzerainty over Tibet. Thus, the principal parties—China, British India and Russia—had accepted Chinese overlordship in Tibet. Even Tibet accepted this, except during the 1913-19 period. Suzerainty meant essentially autonomy of Tibet subject to Chinese directions in defence and foreign affairs.

It is argued sometimes that this suzerainty was forced on Tibet by foreign powers. This argument is advanced by some Tibetans in Delhi. This argument is rather thin because even the institution of the Dalai Lama has taken root with Chinese military patronage. Throughout the history of Tibet, the Dalai Lama sought and obtained the Chinese Emperor's umbrella. Even the Dalai Lama as the unquestioned religious-cum-temporal leader of Tibet was made possible by the intervention of the Chinese Emperor. The Dalai Lama represents the Yellow Sect of Buddhism in Tibet.

Before the institution of Dalai Lama was established, the Red Sect flourished in Tibet. The Red Sect was actually created under the influence of Padmasambhava, also known as Guru Rimpoche. This guru went to Tibet after Shanta Rakshita returned to India unable to tame the "wild Tibetans." Buddhism arrived in Tibet long before the institution of Dalai Lama came into existence. According to Fa Hsien, the Chinese Buddhist traveller to India in the 5th century, Buddhism was established in Han China years before Christ.

But in Tibet, Buddhism came later, in the 7th century. In China, the Yuan dynasty founded by Kublai Khan in 1271 A.D., promoted Buddhism vigorously. It was Kublai Khan who unified Tibet under the Sagya sect (the Red Sect). The Yuan dynasty ended in mid-14th century, and in its place came the Ming dynasty (1368-1644). This coincided with the rise of the Yellow Sect (Gelugba) of Buddhism founded by Zonggaba.

In 1576, Ming prince Anda Khan of Mongolia invited the then Gelugba priest to lecture on Buddhism in Qinghai province. He then declared him a "Rajguru." In 1578, he conferred the title "Holder of Vajra Dalai Lama" on this priest. "Dalai" in Mongolian (not Tibetan word) means "ocean." He was also named the third Dalai Lama. The first and second Dalai Lama were named posthumously; they were the earlier "head priests."

It was the fifth Dalai Lama who formalised Tibet's confederation with ancient China. He sought the Ching dynasty (which replaced the Ming in 1644) intervention for stabilising himself in Tibet. Emperor Shunzhi not only despatched troops to consolidate the Dalai Lama's power, but gave him a gold seal denoting Beijing's recognition. In 1720, with the help of the Chinese Emperor Kang Xi, the King of Tibet was deposed and the ninth Dalai Lama was made political head of Tibet as well. Since then all succeeding Dalai Lamas (the present one in India is the fourteenth) made it the established practice to obtain Beijing's seal of approval to ensure legitimacy as the Dalai Lama. Monarchy came to an end in China in 1911, but the government in Beijing continued its role in Lhasa.

Thus, when on 22 February 1940, the present and 14th Dalai Lama was anointed, a representative of the Chiang Kai-Shek government was especially despatched to Lhasa, and he officiated at the inauguration ceremony. Thus the institution of the Dalai Lama itself has flowered under Chinese umbrella and patronage.

Whenever Tibet looked southward politically, it took aggressive postures. Throughout the nineteenth and twentieth century, Tibet had laid claims to Sikkim, Bhutan and Arunachal. Tawang in Arunachal has always been considered by Tibetans as seat of Tibetan authority. In 1902, Tibetan troops actually invaded Sikkim to capture the area. Lord Curzon ordered a large contingent of the army to go and repulse the Tibetan invasion.

Thus, those who argue for Tibet's independence should be prepared sooner or later consistency—to cede Sikkim, Bhutan and Arunachal Pradesh to Tibet. Is our nation ready for that? Indeed, a perusal of historical records can leave no objective person in doubt that throughout the centuries, Tibet behaved as if its future lay in the overall framework of China. Tibet never once in history had sided with India, even on the legitimacy of the McMahon Line!

Therefore, those who advocate the independence of Tibet, today, do not and cannot argue on the basis of logic of history. Their advocacy unless it is 'red politik', can only be to further political mischief, or to enrich themselves at the nation's cost.

Indian relations with China in 21st century therefore should not be derailed by misconceptions and misplaced adventurism on Tibet that Jawaharlal Nehru engaged in, swinging from one extreme to another extreme in just one decade.

# CHAPTER 2

# The Sino-Indian Border Disputes

## Introduction

The Republic of India and the People's Republic of China, after they came into existence, had faced an unfinished task: How to convert their frontiers into legal boundaries. A Boundary is a geographic line agreed to in diplomatic negotiations (delimitation), jointly marked out on the ground (demarcation), thereafter visualized on a map (cartography), and accurately formalized between two sovereign governments (treaty), in which each thus recognised the limits of its own and that of its neighbour's territory. Such a Sino-Indian boundary never, hitherto, had existed in history.

Bordering fourteen countries, China had claims of lost territories against most of its neighbours. Beijing in the 1950s had thus faced the possibility of quarrels with many of its neighbours particularly with the erstwhile Soviet Union which was the inheritor of vast far eastern tracts of Chinese imperial territory annexed by Tsarist Russia under imposed treaties.

In India, Deputy Prime Minister Sardar Patel had astutely concluded that China would settle its boundaries piecemeal at a time of its choosing. Hence, he had urged Nehru to seize the moment in 1949 and press for a settlement before India recognised the People's Republic of China or promoted her cause in the UN. Zhou Enlai, the Chinese premier, chose at the 1955 Afro-Asian Conference in Bandung to make clear his government's approach to border disputes, which incidentally accorded with Patel's 1950 surmise. Zhou Enlai said:

"With some of our neighbouring countries we have not yet finally fixed our borderline and we are ready to do so. But before doing so, we are willing to maintain the present situation by acknowledging that those parts of our border are parts which are undetermined. We are ready to restrain our government and our people from crossing even one step across our border. If such things do happen, we should like to admit our mistake. As to the determination of common borders which we are going to undertake with our neighbouring countries, we shall use only peaceful means and we shall not permit any other kinds of method. In no case shall we change this."

China negotiated and concluded boundary treaties turn by turn with Burma, Nepal, Pakistan, Afghanistan, Mongolia, Korea, Laos and with Vietnam: In the case of Russia and the Central Asia states of the former Soviet Union negotiations have been completed, and boundaries agreed to subject to caveats on disputes left unresolved for settlement at some indefinite future date.

In the case of the Sino-Soviet border, Moscow had initially refused to renegotiate the 19th century treaties by which the Tsars had annexed the great tracts of the Qing Empire, which became Siberia and the Maritime Province, suspecting that Beijing's insistence on negotiation was with the intention to reclaim that territory. But China's insistence led to armed conflict in 1969, on the Ussuri River banks, and the threat of nuclear war had then loomed on the frontier.

In 1987, under Gorbachev, the USSR however agreed to renegotiate the Sino-Soviet borders. In 1997, the heads of state of Russia and China, met in Beijing, and proclaimed their border settlement as a model for resolving problems left over by history "through negotiations based on equality, mutual understanding and concessions." The Central Asian successor states of the USSR have also followed suit and have now reached settlement on their boundaries with Beijing.

In the case of Vietnam, China under Deng Xiaoping's leadership, had used a minor boundary dispute concerning distances of no more than a few hundred metres, to attack Vietnam to 'teach a lesson'. But now with Vietnam too, the disputes have been resolved.

In comparison to the magnitude of overall China's border problems, the task facing independent India when it emerged from the British rule in 1947, was trivial. Of the six countries with whom India has boundaries, for five when the British handed power over to India, the outstanding issues were settled at the threshold of freedom. Only the border with the then independent Tibet had not been formalized. The attempts of the British governments in London and India to reach agreement in 1914 with China to demarcate the Indo-Tibet boundaries had failed, and these efforts were not revived thereafter for as long as the British remained in India.

## THE MAIN ISSUES OF THE DISPUTE

From a deep perusal of the record of the Sino-Indian border dispute, three clear issues arise:

(I) Did a Sino-Indian border exist at any date before the 1962 border war?

(II) Did the two Prime Ministers of China and India, in particular Zhou Enlai and Jawaharlal Nehru respectively, communicate on the issue honestly and transparently to minimize the danger of armed conflict?

(III) Was there a deeper purpose in the minds of the leadership of the two countries for not resolving the conflict by negotiation in the 1950?.

I. *Did a Sino-Indian border exist at any date before the 1962 border war?*

Britain had convened in Simla in 1913 a tripartite conference, including a Tibetan delegate and a representative of the Chinese central Government, the ostensible purpose of which was to regulate relations between Lhasa and Beijing by demarcating a line to divide inner and outer Tibet as spheres of influence of China and Britain. The British approach to the border was thus that of an imperial power, and not one of defending the Indian nation state. In fact, the British had never had or ranted to consider India as a nation leave alone an ancient and continuing nation in history.

The ruling British view, most famously expressed by John Strachey in his 1888 book was that: "There is not, and never was, an India, or even a country of India, possessing, according to European ideas, any sort of unity—physical, political, social and religious." The then Foreign Secretary of the Indian government, Sir Henry McMahon, however arranged secret and bilateral negotiations in Delhi with Lhasa in March 1914, in which the Tibetan representative was induced to accept a new border line, which came to be named after the Foreign Secretary. It was drawn on a map on a scale of eight miles to the inch, covering the sector from just short of Laos to Bhutan through Burma—which the British had then included as part of their Indian empire.

The Lhasa authorities repudiated their representative's

unauthorized action: The Chinese government, suspecting what had gone on behind its representative's back, declared that any agreement reached between Britain and the Tibetan authorities would be "illegitimate and null." In his report to London, the then Viceroy in India had also disowned McMahon's dealings with the Tibetans. McMahon's actions at Simla thus had also exceeded his authority. The government in London tacitly expressed severe disapproval by transferring McMahon out of India (to Egypt). Thus the 'McMahon Line' was in reality non-starter—till 1936 when in a fraud on history, committed by the British Indian government, the "McMahon Line" made its appearance in official maps.

In the mid-1930s, Olaf Caroe, then a British official in New Delhi, retrieved from the archives documentation concerning the McMahon Line. The British government began thereafter propagating that the McMahon Line was indeed India's legal boundary, claiming it to be legitimized by a formal assent of Tibet and China, for which Caroe arranged a forgery to support the false assertion: that the boundary had been agreed to at the 1913-14 Simla Conference.

Consequently, in the 1940s, some British maps began showing the McMahon Line as the boundary, qualified only with the word: "Undemarcated" (that is, still awaiting agreement on its exact alignment and marking out on the ground by joint inspection process of the two neighbours). During World War II and immediately after it, the Chinese Kuomintang government protested to the interim Indian Government. In early 1947, and even as late as in 1949, the KMT government in China although by then on the way out, still delivered to New Delhi a formal note repudiating all documents emanating from the Simla Conference. On

October 16, 1947, even the Government of Tibet, claiming to be free and independent, sent a note to New Delhi demanding the return of vast tracts of land from Ladakh to Assam!

But on November 20, 1950, Prime Minister Jawaharlal Nehru proclaimed to Parliament that the McMahon Line was indeed India's border with Tibet in the north-west, reiterating that it had been "fixed by the Simla Convention of 1914," even as the Survey of India of the Home Ministry then had published the official map of India showing the border as 'undemarcated' and 'undefined'.

He went on to say "map or no map, the McMahon Line was India's boundary and we will not allow anybody to come across [it]." In February 1951, the Nehru government also annexed Tawang, affirming McMahon who had drawn his line to bring Tawang into India. Lhasa had then vigorously protested India's seizure of Tawang, and again made clear that Tibet regarded the McMahon Line as without validity. And yet the Indian government, ostrich-like began to pretend that there was no dispute on the border, and that there was nothing to discuss about it with China. The sage advice of Patel was ignored, for Nehru to rue later.

India signed the Agreement on Trade and Intercourse in Tibet with China on April 29, 1954, which stated in its preamble the "Five Principles of Peaceful Co-existence: [panchsbee]. No mention in the treaty was made on the finality of the so-called McMahon Line. China also maintained its silence, since as Zhou Enlai was later to say that "the time was not ripe then."

The border dispute between China and India overtly surfaced when China published the completion of a motorable road across Aksai Chin linking Xinjiang with western Tibet.

The Chinese described that "notable engineering feat" in an article on the achievements of their first five-year plan in the July 1958 issue of China Pictorial, and showed it on a map. The Sino-Indian border dispute was thus formally notified by this map and by the subsequent Indian reactions to the same map. Thereafter the relations founded on Panchsheel tumbled for the worse steadily, culminating in a border war between the two giant nations in 1962.

One of the tragic verdicts of research on the Sino-Indian border dispute is that the 1962 armed conflict between the two nations was totally unnecessary. The Indians called the border war as Chinese aggression and perfidy, and the Chinese called it a reply to Indian expansionism and a lesson taught to India. It was neither. It was a war of folly that made two giant neighbours with no fundamental strategic conflict, nor with a history of hostility, to fight a war which had few worthwhile territorial gains of strategic value. But the long-term political consequences for India, which went headlong into the conflict unprepared, has been painful and destabilizing.

For China, the existence of simmering tension with India has kept alive the hope of Tibetan secessionists the world over, that one day, their dream can be true. And considering the Islamic unrest in Xinjiang, Tibet is the soft underbelly of the Chinese dragon, and which unsettled could undermine Chinese security at a future date.

On October 7, 1950, a year after the founding of the People's Republic of China under the presidentship of Mao Ze-dong, Chinese troops entered Tibet. Exactly a month later, on November 7, 1950, Deputy Prime Minister and party heavy weight, Sardar Vallabhbhai Patel wrote a long letter to Prime Minister Jawaharlal Nehru [Appendix I] stating, *inter alia*, the following: "In the background of this, we have to consider what new situation now faces us as a result of the disappearance of Tibet.... We can, therefore, safely assume that very soon they will disown all the stipulations, which Tibet has entered into with us in the past.... The undefined state of the frontier and the existence on our side of a population with its affinities to Tibetans or Chinese have all the elements of potential trouble between China and ourselves."

Sardar Patel then went on to propose to Nehru a 11-point plan to meet the situation which included the need to formulate "the policy in regard to the McMahon Line." All that Sardar Patel had wanted from Nehru was a recognition that since China would soon repudiate all treaties that Tibet had presumed to have signed with India, the undefined state of the frontier called for a "policy on the McMahon line." Instead of a point by point reply which a Deputy Prime Minister was by right entitled, Patel got a lecture on "perspectives" from Nehru. On receipt of this sound advice, Jawaharlal Nehru was obviously irritated.

On foreign policy, Nehru had perhaps thought he had divine wisdom, and this reflected in his reply to Patel dated November 18, 1950. He wrote back rather patronizingly: "If we lose our sense of perspective and world strategy and give way to unreasoning fears, then any policy that we might have is likely to fail."

Sardar Patel had also suggested that before recognising the government of the People's Republic of China, India "might have a discussion in the Cabinet." Nehru replied that such a Cabinet discussion would not be useful because "most members of the cabinet have hardly followed these intricate (diplomatic) conversations and (diplomatic) consultations." Such arrogance blended with ignorance of facts led ultimately to 1962.

Nehru soon thereafter recognised the Chinese sovereignty over Tibet, when all along he had said that India would not go beyond recognising the "suzerainty" of China. Later on one occasion in the late 1950s, he told Nath Pai MP in Parliament that the Chinese language did not distinguish between sovereignty and suzerainty, and therefore in the translation of the Indian Note into Chinese language, an error had crept in: suzerainty was translated as sovereignty. This is entirely face. For centuries the Chinese have used the term tzong funs chuan to describe suzerainty, and jw chuan to denote sovereignty. Unfortunately, nobody then in Parliament knew the Chinese language to expose Nehru's ignorance.

History now affirms that Sardar Patel was right: as Tibet became a province of China—which is what sovereignty meant—all the treaties signed by Tibet stood dissolved, because China repudiated them. Amongst these treaties was the one incorporating the McMahon Line.

In Parliament, on 20 November 1950, Nehru categorically stated that "the frontier from Bhutan eastwards has been clearly defined by the McMahon Line, which was fixed by the Simla Convention of 1914." In this Convention, the Tibetan representative Shatra had signed with India's McMahon.

China had rejected the entire Convention, after withdrawing its representative from the tripartite Simla Conference. This fact had been withheld from the Indian people for a long time even after 1962 till mid-1980s, who had erroneously believed that China was a party to the 1914 Simla Convention.

Nehru's assertion in 1950 in Parliament thus made no legal sense. If Tibet ceased to be independent by our own admission and a subsequent treaty affirmed that (in 1954), then how is an earlier commitment (Simla 1914) with a merged or 'gifted' state (Tibet) still valid if the inheritor state (China) had already disowned the commitments [and in fact when the commitment itself had never been owned, let alone it being disowned]?

Since 1950, Tibet which had earlier during the first four decades of the twentieth century been seen by British Imperialists as a buffer state, was during the Cold War viewed as China's vulnerability or softbelly by the US led anti-Commu-nist crusade. After a hiatus in the 1980s [in the post-cold war period] since 1991, the status of Tibet has become a concern a part of the global campaign on human rights. Tibet thus has been used by governments as the situation demanded, primarily to structure their relations with China, and to embarrass China. India has been unable so far to articulate how it would respond to these international currents. We urgently need to do so now.

However, throughout the modern history of Sino-Indian relations of the twentieth century, the people of both countries have viewed Tibet as a security concern, though the Chinese leadership from the very beginning recognised the geostrategic importance of Tibet, much more clearly than the post-colonial power elite in India had. India instead has been on the defensive on the issue ever since 1950, when Chinese army took over Lhasa. We have patently failed to propound a pro-active consistent policy on Tibet after agreeing to Chinese sovereignty in Tibet.

From 1946 to 1951, Nehru had, *de facto* pursued the same policy as the British did towards Tibet. The two main features of this policy were: (a) treat Tibet as an autonomous buffer state between India and China; (b) recognise Chinese suzerainty but not sovereignty over Tibet i.e., recognize Tibet's autonomy even for treaty-making powers, especially in relation to India.

In 1946, a Tibetan delegation, despite protest from the Kuomintang Chinese delegates, was invited to the Asian Relations Conference in Delhi by Nehru in his capacity as "interim" Prime Minister of British Indian Government. In September 1947 after full independence, the Indian Government wrote to the Lhasa Government stating that all the previous treaty commitments (e.g. Anglo-Tibetan treaties/conventions) would be respected as before.

In 1949, an Indian army officer was sent to Lhasa as adviser to the Tibetan Government. But this inherited policy was casually pursued by Nehru, while Mao, the day the Peoples Republic of China (PRC) was established, pursued China's strategic objectives in Tibet with clear determination and brutal clarity.

Thus after the PLA came into full command of Tibet, which Beijing legitimised by a 17-Point treaty with the Dalai Lama's Government in May 1951, Nehru changed his outlook on Tibet. But, Nehru did not give up on Tibet easily. In 1950, he had tried his best, mainly through diplomacy, to censure the Chinese military occupation of Tibet and strongly advocated "a peaceful resolution" of the problem between China and Tibet.

However, the US and Britain showed scant interest, except as Nehru told Parliament later, to use Tibet to "embarrass China." There was nothing, he had perhaps concluded, thereafter that India could do militarily to dislodge the PLA which was now situated firmly in the trans-Himalayan plateau of Tibet. Therefore, instead of fruitlessly antagonizing Beijing by maintaining the old policy, Delhi should, Nehru may have argued, befriend the 'new China'. This is the most generous construction of Nehru's dilly dallying attitude on Tibet.

After India formally recognised Tibet as part of China in 1954, China's legal claim over Tibet was affirmed. However, on the border question, India had failed to press for a resolution of the border question simultaneously, despite direct nexus of the recognition of Tibet as a province of China with the question. China's claims even today on the border are primarily based on Tibetan documents. Zhou Enlai, in his letter of November 5, 1962 after the 1962 Border War was over, wrote to the Asian and African leaders concerning the Boundary Dispute.

He cited the Tibetan documents to support China's claims. The names of rivers, passes and of other places in the Eastern sector (NEFA/Arunachal Pradesh) were all in Tibetan language. Zhou based China's claims over the Aksai Chin by declaring that it used to be part of Xinjiang and Ngari district of Tibet. In short, China's claims on the border with India are based on Tibetan documents and other Tibetan evidences. Indeed, most of the 245 items of evidence presented by the Chinese side at the 1960 India-China official meetings were Tibetan official documents.

And yet India missed a vital opportunity and the moment of her maximum bargaining position by failing to raise the border question in 1954, when the sovereignty of China over Tibet was by treaty affirmed.

The Sino-Indian Agreement of 1954 thus honed in the basic contradiction in Sino-Indian relations: the unresolved boundary dispute and a resolved Tibetan status. But after its signing, each drew its own silent conclusions to suit their respective interests and rapidly moved to establish their respective claims in the disputed or ill-defined territories. The territorial dispute which the 1954 agreement swept under the carpet was later activated during 1959-62 by domestic events in China, in particular in Tibet, and by the reactions in India, consequences of which neither of the two countries could control.

His Holiness, the Dalai Lama, upon his escape to India (in 1959) addressed the Indian Council of World Affairs, New Delhi, on September 7, 1959, in which he said: "The government of India contends that the boundary between Tibet and India has been finally settled according to the McMahon line, but this boundary was laid down by the Simla convention. And this convention was valid and binding only as between Tibet and the British government.

If Tibet had no international status at the time of conclusion of the convention, it had no authority to enter into such an agreement. Therefore, it is abundantly clear that if you deny the sovereign status of Tibet, you deny the validity of the McMahon line." This elementary logic escaped Nehru till he was rudely awakened to it in 1959. After that, Nehru became captive of events, arid led the country unprepared to the war in 1962. Tibet had unravelled Sino-Indian relations.

It is the central thesis of this book that it is not the Sino-Indian border dispute that is at the core of the unsettled and cyclically rocky Sino-Indian relations, but the unstated and often unarticulated Indian approach to the status of the Tibet and the misperception of India's vague and opaque goals which fuels Chinese misunderstanding of India's intentions.

When the Chinese leaders repeatedly stated that the border dispute can be set aside till 'other issues are sorted out', they are actually indicating that if Tibet's status as a province of China is genuinely accepted by India, then it can be inferred that China would settle the border on India's terms, but not before.

The focal point of Sino-Indian border dispute is whether the boundary, which stretches along about 3,850 kms, had ever been formally delimited. The Chinese stand on the question has been that Sino-Indian border had never been formally delimited, and is disputed. India on the other hand, had contended till 1988, that Sino-Indian border had been delimited through age-old customs, traditions and later in treaties and agreements which India had entered into in 1914 with the Government of Tibet. Hence it cannot be disputed under international law. Since 1988, however the Indian stand has changed: that the border is indeed disputed and should be demarcated by negotiations. This reality dawned late, which reality Rajiv Gandhi as Prime Minister had dared to recognize. However, even he failed to note that crucial nuances of the Chinese perception (see Box on the following page).

When Chinese forces completed their takeover of Tibet, they announced that they did not recognise the treaties and agreements which the Government of Tibet had entered into with India and other neighbouring countries, although the Chinese had no other documentary evidence except Tibetan Government records to support their claims. Even after 1954 when India formally recognised Tibet as a part of China, the Sino-Indian border was not delimited; a second opportunity missed by India. The irony of the Indian contention is that the "treaties and agreements" which India had entered into with independent Tibet were held to be valid, even after Tibet was no more considered independent that it had merged with China, and despite consequently China repudiating any 'imposed' treaty on Tibet.

| | Prime Minister Rajiv Gandhi's view | Prime Minister Li Peng's view |
|---|---|---|
| 1. Assessment, of the visit | "Very good and positive ... has rebuilt friendship between the two countries (Xinhua, 19/12/88)" | "For reasons known as all, unfortunately bilateral relations took a turn for the worse and the deterioration even amounted to confrontation. We hope such things will never happen again" |
| 2. Tibet | "Tibet is a region of China. The Indian Govt. does not allow any political activities harmful to China's internal affairs" (Xinhua, 19/12/88) | The Chinese side express concern over anti-China activities by some Tibetans elements in India" (Xinhua, 23/12/88) |
| 3. Border | "An atmosphere of claim and tranquility along the border should be maintained" (Xinhua, 19/12/88) | "The Boundary problem is hindering the improvement of bilateral relations" (Xinhua, 19/12/88) |

*Note:* It is, thus, clear from the above that Rajiv Gandhi's perception of his visit was entirely optimistic, while the Chinese view in content and tone, was patronizing and cold.

In fact, because of these unstated and unarticulated approaches, the history of Sino-Indian border dispute since 1949 is a history of Jawaharlal Nehru's unforgivable contradictions in public posture and private persuasion that was passed off as Indian Government policy.

Worse, Nehru took these contradictory stances on the Sino-Indian border dispute throughout his tenure as Prime Minister. In the end, he deceived himself, and the country felt that it had been let down by Nehru. How could any Government take the view that on the one hand the McMahon line was the immutable official boundary because of the 1914 Simla Convention. which China had then itself rejected, and on the other hand, Tibet is and was a province of China? Nehru thus should have heeded Patel's warning that because the Government of China had in 1914 refused to agree to be a signatory to the Simla convention, therefore Nehru in 1950 should have demanded a price for agreeing to recognise the sovereignty of China over Tibet. He should have asked the Chinese leadership to clarify its position on the McMahon line.

If the Chinese can accept the McMahon Line in *toto* with Burma, why not with India provided we had then negotiated with our eyes open. This is what Sardar Patel had wanted, but Nehru was too wrapped up in his "perspectives" of world affairs to care. Nehru was shattered by 1962 subsequently, but he has not been yet held accountable by history for this blunder that has cost the nation enormously.

As we have noted above, while Nehru was discoursing in 1950 on the fixity of the McMahon line in Parliament, the Survey of India, the Government of India's official cartographer, published in the same year a map titled: "Political Divisions in the New Republic of India," showing the border along the McMahon line as "undemarcated," and the Aksai Chin area as "boundary undefined". Obviously, the

Home Ministry in which the Survey of India's office was housed was unaware of the External Affairs Ministry's stand, and in turn the Prime Minister was in the dark about his own Government's maps!

Much later, when Nehru moved a resolution in Parliament, on 8 November 1962 (the resolution became famous because MPs had stood up to take an oath "to drive the aggressors out"), he misinformed the House even on the true position of the 1914 convention. He said in the Lok Sabha on that occasion: "Even if the Chinese did not accept it (the McMahon line)—and I would like to say that the objection they raised in 1913 was not based on their objection to the McMahon line, it was based on their objection to another part of the treaty which divided inner Tibet and outer Tibet, the McMahon line did not come in that."

This statement of Nehru is false on the following two grounds. First, the Chinese did object to all the boundary lines drawn by Sir Henry McMahon. On 13 June 1914, about three weeks before McMahon initialed the Simla convention with Tibet's plenipotentiary Lonchen Shatra, Sun Pao-chi, China's foreign minister, handed a memorandum to the British ambassador in Beijing protesting, inter alia, the McMahon line (then called the red line because it was marked by McMahon in red pencil).

The British Ambassador, Sir John Newell Jordan communicated on 16 June 1914 Sun's memorandum to Sir Edward Grey, British foreign secretary in London, in the following words: "I have the honour to forward translation of the memorandum handed to me by Sun Pao-chi, Minister for Foreign Affairs, on the 13th instant, together with copy of a map showing the boundaries of inner and outer Tibet as proposed by Sir Henry McMahon (red and blue), as now proposed by the Chinese government between inner and outer Tibet, as first put by the Chinese at conference (yellow)." Therefore the Chinese objection was not merely the boundary between inner and outer Tibet as Nehru told Parliament but boundaries of outer Tibet (red line) as well, which included the so called McMahon line. Second, if indeed Britain had taken the Simla Convention of 1914 as final, then why did the Imperial power refrain from publishing these maps for 22 years, till 1936?

The Survey of India published official maps in 1917, three years after the Simla convention. In that map, the McMahon line, is not shown. Instead the "traditional" border along the Assam Himalayan foothills below the Tawang tract, and well below the McMahon line is shown.

In 1929, the Encyclopaedia Britannica published its 14th edition. In it the map of the Indo-Tibet border was also published. Volume 24 shows the same "traditional" boundary—below Tawang—and not the line determined 15 years earlier by McMahon. Were these facts not known to Nehru?

One interesting question is why did the British authorities not implement Sir Henry McMahon's "agreement" reached with Tibet's Lonchen Shatra. Incidentally, it is quite significant that all the three plenipotentiaries at the Simla Convention of India, Tibet and China—were sent into disgrace by their respective governments soon after the conference. The Chinese representatives, Chen I-fen (also called Ivan Chen) was disgraced because he had initialed the maps without his government's sanction. The Chinese Government had promptly disowned it.

In fact, Chen was suspected of being a British lackey if not an agent. In a secret telegram sent on 20 August 1911, Sir John Jordan, the British ambassador in Beijing had stated: "It is a decided gain to have a man like Ivan Chen on the frontier." The Tibetan representative Lonchen Shatra was also sent into obscurity because of his signing away Tawang to McMahon. Ironically, the man who did the most for British India, Sir Henry McMahon, was immediately transferred to Egypt, which was the British bureaucracy's way of expressing displeasure. This was in sharp contrast to the lionising he was privy to in London after McMahon's earlier venture in Afghanistan. Britain refused even to acknowledge the existence of his maps for 22 years thereafter.

Why did the British react in this manner? One reason was that Britain did not want to, for inches of Indian territories on a map, jeopardise its commercial interests in China. The Manchu dynasty had been overthrown in 1911, and Yuan Shihkai had become President of China. Yuan was being wooed by the British, and they did not want to annoy him. Besides, in negotiating with the Tibetans, Sir Henry McMahon was flouting instructions from London, and going beyond his brief which disobedience was a monumental crime in British bureaucracy.

Thus, the secretary of state for India, Robert Crewe-Milnes, had sent a telegram to Viceroy Hardinge on 1 July 1914, just two days prior to the signing of the Simla Convention, as follows:

"Conference regarding Tibet. Please refer to your telegram dated the 29th. A final meeting of the conference should be summoned by Sir H. McMahon on the 3rd July. If the Chinese plenipotentiary then refuses to sign, negotiations should definitely he terminated by Sir Henry. He should express to the Tibetan representative great regret at failure to arrive at a settlement and should also assure Lonchen Shatra that Tibet may depend on diplomatic support of His Majesty's government and on any assistance in the way of munitions of war which we can give them, if aggression on part of China continues."

McMahon was not authorised to sign any agreement with Tibet in the absence of Chinese concurrence. This was also the commitment of Britain in the Anglo-Russian Convention of 1907. Just in case Viceroy Hardinge had still remained in doubt, Crewe-Milner sent another telegram on 3 July 1914: "With reference to your telegram of the 2nd instant, separate signature with Tibet cannot be authorised by His Majesty's government. Sir H. McMahon should proceed in the manner laid down in my telegrams dated, respectively, the 1st and 2nd July, if the Chinese delegate refuses to sign." But disregarding these instructions, McMahon went ahead and initialed an 11-Article Convention on 3 July 1914 with the Tibetans, in clear violation of the Anglo-Russian Convention of 1907.

Lord Hardinge, however, had been indulgent with McMahon. He had in telegrams to Crewe-Milner frequently referred to how the Russians by being tough with the Chinese were getting their way in Mongolia. However, even he had to say the following while forwarding McMahon's memorandum to London on 23 July 1914: "... We recognise that a consideration of the eastern or Indo-Chinese portion of the north-eastern frontier did not form part of the functions of the conference, and we would therefore request that the views and proposals put forward may be regarded as per-sonal to Sir Henry McMahon, and not at present carrying the endorsement of the government of India.

Sir Henry McMahon was able to get away from being cashiered from services for flouting instructions, by using the age-old bureaucratic device of finding contradictions in instructions from London and in "not having time for references." He has recorded in his memorandum regarding progress of negotiations from 1 May to 8 July 1914 that: "I was somewhat uncertain however as to the exact intention of His Majesty's government in regard to final action.... There was no time for a further reference to London, and I accordingly decided that if the Chinese plenipotentiary refused to cooperate at the last moment, I would not sign with Tibet, but would initial the amended Convention and map in concert with my Tibetan colleague."

Therefore, the so-called McMahon line, which Nehru had referred to in every discussion on the Sino-Indian border question, has no legal validity arising from any Agreement or Convention that is binding on the Government of China. One could have stretched the initialing of the 1914 memorandum as a binding agreement, but the day we accepted the sovereignty of China over Tibet, even that flimsy basis evaporated.

The initialing of the Simla Convention maps by Sir Henry McMahon and Lonchen Shatra of Tibet, was in violation of the Anglo-Russian convention of 1907 by which Britain had agreed not to deal with Tibet except through the intermediary of China. Hence even that was of no use to India's case based on McMahon Line. India does have an argument, though. But we shall reserve that for later in this book. For the moment, it suffices to say that China too has no case.

The British Government refused to acknowledge the existence of the McMahon line till 1936. Between 1914 and

1933, nothing had happened to change this attitude of the British government. However in 1933, the 13th Dalai Lama "attained the heaven." The Kuomintang government despatched General Huang Mu-sung with a high-powered delegation to Lhasa to mourn his death. The delegation carried enough gold to bribe the whole of Tibet, and stayed in Lhasa for six months "to mourn" the Dalai Lama's death. This scared the British in India. General Huang also obtained a reaffirmation from the Tibetans, of Chinese suzerainty over Tibet.

In 1935, a British botanist, Kingdon Ward, was arrested by the Tibetans because he entered Lhasa via Tawang. They argued that he needed Tibetan authorised papers even to pass through the Tawang tract. The Foreign and Political Department of the Government of India (fore runner of the Ministry of External Affairs) was entrusted with the case of Ward's release. Deputy Secretary, Olaf K. Caroe (later knighted), therefore called for the files. Perusal of the files enabled Caroe to stumble on the McMahon-Shatra agreement on the McMahon line which made Tawang Tract Indian territory. Years later, Sir Olaf Caroe [421 recorded in a journal article the following: "The McMahon line was drawn just before World War I, and then forgotten, and I know all about this because it was I who discovered that it had been forgotten."

To bolster their case vis-a-vis the arrest of Kingdon Ward, the Government of British India, on the prodding of a Deputy Secretary, decided to pursue with His Majesty's government in London the need to accord official sanction to the McMahon line, and with retrospective effect! Official public sanction of treaties, maps, etc. were given in those days by a publication called Collection of Engagements, Treaties and Sanads, under the editorship of C.U. Aitchison, and published under the authority of the Foreign and Political Department, Government of India. These Aitchison volumes had been appearing at 15 years intervals, but without any reference to the McMahon line.

In 1929, Volume XIV of the Aitchison Treaties made no reference to the McMahon line, but it contained a paragraph about the Simla Convention of 1914, and the attempt to settle boundaries of Inner Tibet, i.e., the Sino-Tibetan frontier (but not outer Tibet, i.e., the Indo-Tibetan border). It also records the Chinese government's refusal to sign the Convention.

Sir Olaf Caroe's attention naturally moved from the files to the Aitchison volumes, with the object of obtaining official recognition to the "forgotten" convention. So Caroe wrote to the India Office in London seeking permission to make public the 1914 Convention and incorporate the maps in the Aitchison Treaties. In his letter dated April 19, 1936, addressed to the Assistant Under Secretary of State for India, John Walton, Caroe argued thus: "... The government of India think there would be advantage in inserting in their public records copies of the 1914 Convention. Their absence from such a publication as 'Aitchinson's Treaties,' if it became known to the Chinese government, might well be used by them in support of the argument that no ratified agreement between India and Tibet is in existence."

On June 4, 1936, Walton recorded an India Office minute, in which he cited the "risk of attracting unwelcoming Chinese notice" as the reason for non-publication of the 1914 papers and maps. Then in a subsequent India Office minute dated

September 9, 1936, he recorded: The juridical position in regard to the north-east frontiers is not perfectly secure, because the agreements of 1914 on the subject were concluded only with Tibet and not with China, and China has an acknowledged claim to suzerainty over Tibet."

But other pressures to publish the 1914 maps emerged. The Government of India Act of 1935 required a precise delineation of tribal Assam. The impending separation of Burma similarly required precise descriptions of the boundary. Caroe used this pressure to press his arguments. He said: "... While the Burma government were informed of the location of this frontier (McMahon line), the Assam government apparently were forgotten and seem to have had no intimation upto this day...." Sir Olaf Caroe won his point. But the British government urged him to include the 1914 Convention documents in the Aitchison Treaties "unobtrusively" and with "minimum publicity." London also wanted the Government of India to bring out a revised edition of the "Aitchison Treaties," and withdraw and call back the earlier editions that were in circulation.

All this suited Caroe very well. He quietly ordered the withdrawal of the old set of "Aitchison Treaties" and re-printed a fresh set in 1938, but fraudulently with a 1929 dateline. This was entirely unethical, but Caroe went even further. He replaced the short factual paragraph about the 1914 Convention, with a long embellished three-paragraph set. He also included as many favourable references for British India as was synoptically feasible [see Box below]. This act was not only immoral but a crime of forgery as well under the Indian Penal Code.

| (1929) Published Original (available in Widener Library, Harvard University, USA) | (1936) Reprinted and Forged (With the Ministry of External Affairs, New Delhi) |
|---|---|
| In 1913 a conference of Tibetan, Chinese and British Plenipotentiaries met in India to try and bring about a settlement in regard to matters on the Sino-Tibetan frontier; and a tripartite Convention was drawn up initialled in 1914. The Chinese Government, however, refused to permit their Plenipotentiary to proceed to full signature. | In 1913 a conference of British, Chinese and Tibetan Plenipotentiaries was convened in Simla in an attempt to negotiate an agreement as to the inter-national status of Tibet with particular regard to the relations of the three Governments and to to the frontier of Tibet both with China and India. After prolonged negotiations the conference under the presidency of Sir Henry McMahon drew up a tripartite Convention between Great Britain, China and Tibet, which was initialed in Simla in 1914 by the representatives of the three parties. The Chinese Government, however, refused to ratify the agreement, by their refusal depriving them-selves of the benefits which they were to obtain thereunder, among which were a definite recognition that Tibet was under Chinese suzerainty, and an agreement to permit a Chinese official with a suitable escort not exceeding 300 men to be maintained in Lhasa. The Convention was, how-ever ratified by Great Britain and Tibet by means of a declaration accepting its terms as binding as between themselves. The Convention included a definition of boundary |

| | |
|---|---|
| | both on the Sino-Tibetan and the Indo-Tibetan frontier. On the Sino-Tibetan frontier a double boundary was laid down, the portion between the two boundaries being spoken of as Inner Tibet and that part of Tibet lying west of the westerly boundary as Outer Tibet. Owing to the failure of the Chinese Government to ratify, these boundaries, however, remained fluid. The other frontier between India and Tibet on the Assam and Burma borders, which was accepted by His Majesty's Government and the Tibetan Government was laid down between the eastern border of Bhutan and the Isuazi Pass on the Irrawady-Salween water-parting. West of the Brahmaputra bend this frontier for the most part follows the main axis of the Himalayas, and east of that point includes all tribal territory under the political control of Assam and Burma Governments. This frontier throughout stands back some 100 miles from the plains of India and Burma. A new set of Trade Regulations between Great Britain and Tibet were concluded under the Convention to replace the earlier regulations of 1893 and 1908. |

From C.U. Aitchison: Collection of Engagements, Treaties and Sanads [Published under the Authority of the Foreign and

Political Department, Government of India, Vol. XIV (1929)].

The reprinted fraudulent copy then "unobtrusively" replaced the original Aitchison Treaties all over the world (there were only 62 copies originally circulated). In three places however the original copy remained—one in Caroe's office (to become later the Ministry of External Affairs), the second in the India Office library in London, and the third in the Harvard University Widener library. Harvard just refused to part with the original.

Thereafter, the Surveyor General of India was ordered to change the Survey of India maps to incorporate the McMahon line. In 1938 he did so, after pointing out numerous geographic anomalies in this boundary. Even thereafter, the Survey of India maps uptill 1954 showed the McMahon line as "undemarcated," and the Aksai Chin area as "boundary undefined."

In the Ladakh area (the western sector of the frontier), the area in which the Chinese built the Aksai Chin road Nehru had maintained that the Sino-Indian boundary was delimited by the Treaty of 1842 and that in 1847 "the Chinese government admitted that this boundary was sufficiently and distinctly fixed." Furthermore, Nehru had told Parliament that this area "now claimed by China has always been depicted as part of India on official maps, has been surveyed by Indian officials, and even a Chinese map of 1893 shows it as Indian territory." There is no substance to any of these claims.

In the West of Tibet, i.e., the Kashmir frontier, the Indian governments from 1860s have floundered on what line to adopt. In 1841, Sardar Gulab Singh led the Sikhs to Tibet and his General Zorawar Singh captured the Manasarovar-Kailash area. Tibetans with Chinese help, counter-attacked in Leh in Ladakh. But the fierce Sikhs were victorious. In 1842 a treaty was signed between Kashmir, Tibet and China. By that even if the descriptions are vague, Aksai Chin was ceded to India. But the British mutilated that treaty in 1848, after taking over, following the Anglo-Sikh wars of 1846. The status of Aksai Chin since became unclear. On June 10, 1873, a cartographer at the India Office, Trelawney Saunders prepared for the foreign office a map which roughly followed the Karakoram range as the boundary—which every Viceroy till 1899 favoured.

On March 14, 1899, Sir Claude MacDonald, the British Minister in Beijing, delivered a Note to the Chinese Foreign Office proposing a new line "for the sake of avoiding any dispute or uncertainty in the future." It acknowledged that the boundaries of Hunza (in the Northern Areas under Pakistan's control) with China "have never been clearly defined" and suggested that, in that sector, both sides should relinquish their claims on each other [This is precisely what the Sino-Pak agreement of March 2, 1963 is based on]. The Note proceeded to define the boundary eastwards from the Karakoram pass down to "the eastern boundary of Ladakh ... a little east of 80 east longitude." By this line, Aksai Chin became Tibetan.

Thus, emerged the MacDonald-Macartney Line. The Macartney in the hyphenated duo, was George Macartney, the British representative in Kashgar, whose reports to London prodded furious thinking on the boundary and scrapping of Gulab Singh's achievements of 1842. Beijing however did not respond to the offer of 1899. London therefore reverted to a more ambitious one of January 1, 1897 (the Ardagh Line) with various modifications. The long and short of it was that the boundary remained undemarcated.

Thus on the Kashmir frontier, unless the Indian state claims to be the successor to Maharaja Gulab Singh, the status of Aksai Chin is unclear and disputed, thanks to British Imperialists. No wonder, after India achieved independence in 1947, the then government of Tibet sent a protest Note demanding vast tracts of Aksai Chin (up to Assam).

Sardar Patel thus had been right all along in urging Nehru to formulate a policy with regard to the "undefined state of our frontier." In 1952, Girija Shankar Bajpai, former foreign secretary and then Governor of the old Bombay state, wrote to Nehru, following Patel's line of caution. He said that for China, the McMahon line might be one of those "scars left by Britain in the course of her aggression against China (who) may seek to heal or erase the scar on the basis of frontier rectifications that may not be either to our liking or interest."

Nehru had replied to Bajpai: "It is not in India's interest to raise the question of the McMahon line. And if the Chinese raised the issue, we can take our stand that there is nothing to discuss about it." Bajpai wrote back that the Chinese have "no intention of raising it until it suits their convenience." He once again urged Nehru to raise the border question with the Chinese because then India would at least know where it stood. His sound advice too fell on deaf ears.

Nehru not only brushed aside the sober advice but declared in Parliament on 20 November 1950: "Map or no map, McMahon line is our definitive border, and no one will be allowed to cross that frontier." Nehru learnt exactly 22 years later to his cost that he was wrong on both counts. McMahon line was not a definitive border at all, and Nehru could not stop the Chinese from crossing it.

II. *Did the two Prime Ministers of China and India, in particular Zhou Enlai and Jawaharlal Nehru respectively, communicate on the issue honestly and transparently to minimize the danger of armed conflict?*

Sino-Indian friendship, however was terminally wounded in the autumn 1959 when China and India fought their first border battle in Longju, then in Kongka Pass, and was finally laid to rest in 1962. On August 25, 1959 Chinese troops crossed the McMahon line in the NEFA area and exchanged fire with Indian troops already stationed at Longju. India reported one soldier killed and dozen wounded. Although the Indian and Chinese versions of the Longju incident differed, it was clear that this incident soured the relations.

Almost two months later the Chinese troops exchanged fire at the Kongka pass, both sides suffering casualties. It should be noted that even by the time of the Longju incident in August, the Chinese had not made any official claim regarding the McMahon Line or the Ladakh area. It was on September 26, 1959, when Premier Zhou [in a letter to Premier Nehru] finally made an official claim that the McMahon Line was illegal and invalid, and claimed that the international boundary was below the mountains.

Nehru wrote back to Chou expressing his great "surprise and distress" over the latter's letter on September 26, 1959. Referring to the McMahon Line as the boundary in the eastern area of the frontier, Nehru stated:

"When I discussed this with you, I thought we were confronted with the problem of reaching an agreement on where exactly the so-called McMahon Line in the eastern section of the boundary lay. Even when I re-ceived your letter of July 23, 1959, I had no idea that the People's Republic of

China would lay claim to about 40,000 square miles of what in our view has been indisputably Indian territory for decades and in some sectors for over a century."

And then Nehru added:

"We did not release to the public the information which we had about the various border intrusions into our territory by various Chinese personnel since 1954, the construction of a road across Indian territory in Ladakh, and the arrest of out personnel in the Aksai Chin area in 1958 and their detention. We did not give publicity to this in hope that peaceful solutions of the disputes could be furthered."

There cannot be an admission of a Prime Minister that is so self-condemnatory.

It is difficult to believe that officials such as Girija Shankar Bajpai would, after Independence, not have at least orally briefed Nehru about the fraud on maps committed by Sir Olaf Caroe. But Nehru, without getting the border issues clarified and settled with China, instead took the path of deception. "We need not raise the question of our frontier," he wrote to Sheikh Abdullah on August 25, 1952, "but if we find that the Chinese maps continue to indicate that part of our territory is on their side, then we shall have to point this out to the Chinese Government. We need not do this immediately, but we should not put up with this for long and the matter have to be taken up."

Nehru's ambivalence on China and deception with the Indian public had obviously continued, and so he did little—till the Chinese rudely woke him up to it. Nehru should have known that the Chinese coyness on the border question was not oversight at all.

On June 16, 1952, Nehru had wired India's Ambassador to China, K.M. Panikkar that: "We think it is rather odd that in discussing Tibet with you (on June 14) Zhou Enlai did not refer at all to our frontier. For our part, we attach more importance to this than to other matters, and we have made it perfectly clear in Parliament that these frontiers must remain. There is perhaps some advantage in our not raising this issue. On the other hand, I do not quite like Zhou Enlai's silence about it when discussing even minor matters."

This was how Nehru conducted the affairs of the state! Obviously Zhou and Nehru were playing poker—the Chinese way. Nehru was the novice, the Zhou the consummate inscrutable artiste.

Panikkar persuaded Nehru not to press the border issue. By his long epistles to Nehru, he managed to get Nehru to reply: "In view of what you say, it will be desirable not to raise the question of our frontier at this stage." Panikkar was not accountable to the people, but Nehru was. He should have taken the nation into confidence on the true state of the border.

Nehru however also remained confused. In a Note to his Foreign Secretary (July 25, 1952) he wrote: "I appreciate the reasons which Panikkar advanced.... But I am beginning to feel that our attempt at being clever might overreach itself (sic.). I think it is better to be absolutely straight and frank."

On September 6, 1952, Nehru further wrote to the Foreign Secretary, affirming that: "On reconsideration, I accept Panikkar's advice that we should not make specific mention about the frontiers." What made Nehru become ostrich like, few have a clue even today. He never consulted his Cabinet on this subject till 1960. Nehru was confused, adamant and also practised deception on this issue.

In a minute of May 12, 1954, just after signing the Sino-Indian Agreement in Tibet, Nehru wrote: "I agree that we should establish check-posts at all disputed (sic.) points wherever they may be." Thus, the ill-famed 'Forward Policy' was not the outcome or reaction to the Chinese incursions of 1959-60 as is commonly assumed but a premeditated design of the Nehru as early as 1954. That it proved to be counterproductive later is another matter.

Some further dates now bear recalling to provide the total context: On June 18, 1954, Nehru sent a 'Note on Tibet and China' to the Secretary-General, the Foreign Secretary, and Joint Secretary of Ministry of External Affairs. He wrote:

"No country can ultimately rely upon the permanent goodwill or bonafides of another country, even though they might be in close friendship with each other. It is not inconceivable that China and the Soviet Union may not continue to be as friendly as they are now. Certainly it is conceivable that our relations with China might worsen, although there is no immediate likelihood of that..., Adequate precautions have to be taken. If we come to an agreement with China in regard to Tibet, that is not a permanent guarantee." Nehru added: "Of course, both the Soviet Union and China are expansive. They are expansive for evils other than communism, although communism may be made a tool for the purpose. Chinese expansionism has been evident during various periods of Asia history for a thousand years or so. We are perhaps facing a new period of such expansionism...."

On July 1, 1954, Nehru further despatched a 17 para Memorandum to his officials, which contained an important directive to publish new maps! Paras 7 to 10 of this Memorandum contains it all:

"7. All our old maps dealing with this frontier should be carefully examined and, where necessary, withdrawn. Neu) maps should be printed showing our Northern and North Eastern frontier without any reference to any 'line'. These new maps should also not state there is any undemarcated territory. The new maps should be sent to our Embassies abroad, should be introduced to the public generally and be used in our schools, colleges, etc.

8. Both as flowing from our policy and as consequence of our Agreement with China, this frontier should be considered firm and definite one which is not open to discussion with anybody. There may be very minor points of discussion. Even these should not be raised by us. It is necessary that the system of check-posts should be spread along this entire frontier. More especially, we should have check-posts in such places as might be considered disputed areas.

9. Our frontier has been finalised not only by implication in this Agreement but the specific passes mentioned are direct recognitions of our frontier there. Check-posts are necessary not only to control traffic, prevent unauthorised infiltration but as symbols of India's frontier. As Demchok is considered by the Chinese as a disputed territory, we should locate a check-post there. So also at Tsang Chokia.

10. In particular, we should have proper check-posts along the Tibet border and on the passes etc. leading to Jothi Math, Badrinath, etc."

Thus, it is highly puzzling that Nehru publicly postured to befriend China, but his confidential minutes, notes and memos were postured on aggressive intentions which paradoxically were not matched by commitment to military preparedness and expenditure. Under the 1954 trade agreement, the Government of India had unilaterally handed over all of India's extra-territorial rights in Tibet acquired in 1914, to China.

The argument put forth by Nehru was that these rights were acquired by the British through imperialism. Then was not the McMahon line a product of the same imperialism? The Indian case on the border became riddled with such contradiction which made its case look ridiculous in any international forum. The pragmatic policy in 1954 would have been to incorporate a negotiated border settlement with the trade agreement as a price for giving up the rights India had acquired in Tibet through' the 1914 Convention, a price India failed to extract earlier—first at the time (in 1949) of recognition of the People Republic (1950), and second, while proposing that China replace Taiwan in the UN Security Council and General Assembly (in 1951).

Instead, the government of India not only lost vital leverages for final settlement, but took the matter to the ludicrous limit by secretly revising the 1950 Survey of India map in 1954, and arbitrarily drawing the Kashmir (Aksai Chin sector) and NEFA borders as if it had already been defined and demarcated. Thus, through bureaucratic sleights-of-hand, first in 1914, then in 1936, and finally in 1954, the government of India defined a Sino-Indian border without the other side's concurrence. Such 'definition' of a border is unparalleled in the history of modern nations.

In October 1954, when Nehru visited China, nothing was said in public about the undefined border. However, Nehru later recorded in his letter to Zhou [dated 14 December 1958], that he had raised with him the question of "wrong maps" published in China, and according to Nehru, Zhou had told him that "these maps are reproductions of old pre-liberation maps and (China) had no time to revise them." Zhou Enlai however in his reply [dated 8 September 1959] wrote:

"Nevertheless since China and India have not delimited their mutual boundary through friendly negotiations and joint surveys, China has not asked India to revise its maps. In 1954, I explained to your excellency for the same reason that it would be inappropriate for the Chinese government to revise the old maps right now."

While Nehru can be faulted for not raising the border question earlier, Zhou should have by then known of the new 1954 Survey of India map. This was not an old map of India's but a freshly revised one. Why did not Zhou Enlai raise a protest with Nehru? On the contrary, Nehru revealed in his [14 December 1958] letter that: "I remember your telling me that you did not approve of this border being called the McMahon line.... You told me then that you had accepted this McMahon line border with Burma and, whatever might have happened long ago, in view of the friendly relations which existed between China and India, you propose to recognise this border with India also." Nehru then goes on to add: "I had thought then of writing to you on this subject, but I decided not to trouble you over such a petty (sic) matter."

"Petty matter" it was not! Nehru's failure to write a for-mal letter in 1956 to Zhou was a costly error, but Zhou also failed to record his government's stand then in writing despite knowing of 1954 Survey of India map. These lapses then built up the atmosphere of distrust. Zhou Enlai in his reply [dated 23 January 1959] made the following amazing admission: "It was true that the border question was not raised in 1954 when negotiations were being held between Chinese and Indian sides for the agreement on trade and intercourse between the Tibet region of China and India. This was because conditions were not yet ripe for its settlement." This admission clearly means that Zhou led Nehru up the garden path, and Nehru too was naive enough to tread that path.

Nehru in his letter of August 21, 1958 to Zhou Enlai recalled that such cartographic contradictions had been raised in discussion with Zhou Enlai when he had visited China in 1954 but had been reassured that "current Chinese maps were based on old maps" and that the People's Republic "had no time to correct them." The letter concluded with an offer, which seem deliberatively offensive, to send a free copy of the latest Indian official map to guide Beijing's cartographers. The sting in Nehru's letter lay in the last sentence: "There can be no question of these large part of India [shown as within China on Chinese maps] being anything but India and there is no dispute about them."

Zhou replied to these two letters of Nehru in January 1959. In summary, his points were: (1) The Sino-Indian boundary had never been formally delimited. That is, no treaty or agreement on the boundary had even been concluded between the Chinese central government and a government of India. (2) Border disputes (did) exist between China and India and therefore it was unavoidable that there would be discrepancies between their respective maps. (3) The Aksai Chin area was China's and had always been under Chinese jurisdiction. (4) The McMahon Line had no legitimacy as an international boundary but China was likely to accept that alignment at the appropriate time and circumstances, as it was doing in the negotiations with Burma.

Nehru then invited Zhou to India to discuss the border issue. Zhou came in 1960, while China was in the middle of its worst internal crisis since 1949, arising out of the failure of the Great Leap Forward, the worst drought in the century claiming

16 to 32 million deaths in famine, the near collapse of the industrial system clue to the sudden pull out of Soviet engineers with their blue prints from 160 major industrial projects under turn-key collaboration agreements, and the party crisis with the sacking of the Defence Chief Peng Dehuai and the rise of Liu Shaochi as the new President of China, challenging chairman Mao after succeeding him as head of state.

Following six days of talks between the Indian Prime Minister Jawaharlal Nehru and the Chinese Premier Zhou Enlai in April 1960, the latter in a press conference made six points: These were:

1. That the two sides accept that there is a dispute;

2. There is a Line of Actual Control upto which both sides exercise jurisdiction;

3. In determining boundaries geographical principles like watersheds ought to be applicable on all sectors;

4. A settlement of the boundary ought to take into account the national feelings of the people of the two countries to the Himalayas and Karakorams;

5. Pending settlement both sides should recognise LAC and not put forward territorial claims as preconditions but individual adjustments can be made; and

6. In order to ensure peace and tranquillity both sides should refrain from patrolling all sectors of the boundary.

Thirty years later in 1990, India in the second meeting of the Joint Working Group (set up in 1988) held in Delhi in August 1990, told the Chinese that it accepted there was indeed a border dispute; that it was willing to negotiate an entirely new alignment to the Sino-Indian border, thirdly, India had possible alignment proposal [which the Indian government put forth in 1993].

From the points put across by the Indian Government side now it would seem that the "ideal" border line would approximate the Line of Actual Control on September 7, 1962 or a mutually accepted date prior to the outbreak of the Sino-Indian border war of October 1962. Between 1960 and 1985, the Chinese negotiation position was of trading off their claim in the East with the Indian claim in the West. This was in reality to ratify the status quo, or alternatively, set to aside the question, and settle other issues of contention.

For China, border or tracts of land was not the issue but India's perceived goals in Tibet which perception had been inflamed by Nehru's ambiguity, and the growing Indian opposition led by Ram Manohar Lohia and his disciples. Lohia was clear if impractical. Nehru may have had an instinctively practical attitude to Tibet, but it was dented by ambiguity, deception and doubt. He in the end, landed India into the worst of both alternatives. Contrast Nehru's letter of March 22, 1959 to Zhou with the subsequent Indian position since 1988:

"Contrary to what has been reported to you, this line (McMahon Line) was, in fact, drawn at a Tripartite Conference held at Simla in 1913-14 between the Plenipotentiaries of the governments of China, Tibet and India. At the time of acceptance of the delineation of this frontier, Lonchen Shatra, the Tibetan Plenipotentiary, in letters exchanged, stated explicitly that he had received orders from Lhasa to agree to the boundary as marked on the map appended to the Convention. The line was drawn after full discussion and was confirmed subsequently by a formal exchange of letters; and there is nothing to indicate that the Tibetan authorities were in any way dissatisfied with the agreed boundary. Moreover, although the Chinese Plenipotentiary at the Conference objected to the boundaries between Inner and Outer Tibet and between Tibet and China there is no mention of any Chinese reservation in respect of the India-Tibet frontier either during the discussions or at the time of their initialing the Convention. In our previous discussions and particularly during your visit to India in January 1957, we were gratified to note that you were prepared to accept this new line as representing the frontier between China and India in this region and I hope that we shall reach an understanding on this basis."

This was clearly a false understanding of the records in the Government of India's position, and which falsity Nehru ought to have known. It is, thus not possible to give him the benefit of doubt on this matter. Hence, on the first issue, it is clear that a legal defined Sino-Indian border never had existed. It is to the credit of Rajiv Gandhi that he corrected for the mendacity of his grandfather on this issue, even if history has yet to judge Nehru on it. China may have led him up the garden path, but there was no excuse for Nehru to tread it.

It is thus time that the myth about an "idealistic" Nehru with "romantic" notions about China, of being "deceived" by that country, is exploded because deception albeit in a confused way was practised equally by Nehru. Sheikh Abdullah's dismissal for example, from the 'Premiership' of Kashmir on August 8, 1953, and his imprisonment for long years was indeed on Nehru's directive, inspite of his repeated denial. Two notes of July 31, 1953 to M.O. Mathai and the Intelligence Bureau (I.B.) Director B.N. Mullick and other materials leave no doubt that Nehru had ordered it, although he had flatly denied the fact in writing to the President (August

9), to Parliament (August 10), the Chief Ministers (August 22), and worst of all, even to his daughter, Indira Gandhi (August 29)! Nehru had erred on China not bn the score of appeasement but feigned self-righteousness, by treating India as if it was his family silver. This approach governed his policies in Kashmir as well. But the Chinese were better and smarter in the art of deception. In 1962, Nehru paid for his folly. India lost its artificial international status and Nehru was exposed as a "paper tiger."

The decision to "evict" China from Indian territory by force was officially stated on October 12, 1962 when Nehru announced at a press conference at the Delhi airport that he had ordered the Indian army "to drive the Chinese out from NEFA." Three days later his Defence Minister, Krishna Menon, confirmed the decision: "We will fight to the last man, to the last," he pompously told a party gathering.

This set the course for open warfare, but China, was ready and prepared. India was not. The People's Daily, [October 14, 1962] advised Nehru to "pull back from the brink of the precipice," an ominous warning which Nehru ignored. Thus, China, well prepared to wage an offensive war, decided to strike first on October 20, and strike hard. It was India, despite its "forward policy" adventurism, which was unprepared for the contingency of a massive wave of Chinese armed personnel across the Himalayas. That obvious contingency obtaining was what let India down, for which Nehru and Krishna Menon bear the most responsibility.

At the end of the 1961, there were in the western sector, instead of five regular battalions that was required; only one regular battalion and two militia battalions with almost no artillery deployed. As a result, in the summer of 1961 the

Indian army maintained in the western sector a series of military posts and positions that for the most part, except in the Damchuk area, did not even reach the border line claimed by the Chinese. On the other hand, the Chinese in the western sector had a network of roads and a military force the size of a division, including armoured components.

Therefore, in a letter in April 1961 to the Minister of Defence, the Indian Army Chief wrote: "As things stand today it has to be accepted that should the Chinese wish to carry out strong incursions into our territory at selected points, we are not in a position to prevent them from doing so." Along the northern border, the ratio of forces was five to one in favour of the Chinese, whose units were concentrated together, while those of the Indian army were scattered over a wide area with hardly any communications or manageable supply routes between them. There were units which could only receive supplies from the air and were dependent on the weather and the pilot's ability to make their drops accurately; ground conditions made the retrieval of inaccurately dropped supplies almost impossible. The air force was thus under constant pressure to over-stretch its transport capacity. Field officers in the Eastern Command suggested concentrating Indian forces at potential invasion points in the eastern sector.

This would have solved a large number of the logistical problems and would have forced the Chinese to fight where India chose. Moreover, sitting on the McMahon Line itself allowed only backwards manoeuver unless India had wished to invade Tibet. But this suggestion, which was both tactically and strategically wise, had become impossible politically. Nehru (New Delhi) thought it essential to demonstrate a military presence in the entire area.

From a logistical point of view the army was unable to supply its soldiers with suitable personnel equipment and provisions for Himalayan conditions. The Indian soldier was for example, issued a gun dating from World War II in 1962, the army was short of 60,000 automatic rifles, 700 anti-tank weapons, at least 2,000 light mortars, artillery ammunition, 5,000 communication sets, 36,000 radio batteries and 2,000 light trucks. Two tank regiments were paralysed due to lack of spare parts, and aircrafts grounded for the same reason.

The level of training and the morale of troops were also in a deplorable state. The Indian Army was by and large, a plain's army trained and equipped accordingly. Its past conventional warfare had been in the north-west frontier. As early as the beginning of the 1950s, army commanders thought that they should prepare for the possibility of an attack from the north, and plans were made to issue a volume dealing with tactics, strategies, organisation and equipment of the Chinese infantry. Nehru, however, shelved the idea from fear of seeming to provoke China.

At the end of 1960s, the Army Chief who had visited Switzerland to observe the training procedures, organisation and equipment of Alpine divisions, on his return proposed the establishment of a number of mountain divisions to be supported by a motorised force whose regular base would be at the foot of the Himalayas. This suggestion was rejected by Nehru on the grounds that India could not take on unjustified expenditures. There were few officers trained in mountain combat, a position that remained so till the end of 1962.

Nehru had never been to the disputed area, and was dazzled and impressed by the maps shown to him by sycophantic senior army men, on which the dozens of new positions established were marked on these maps as part of the Forward Policy. But on the map, the terrain did not look as forbidding as it was in reality. On a map distances are measured by kilometres, but in the mountain they are measured by days. It is no wonder thus that Nehru fell victim to his own illusions.

Nehru, in Parliament and in other forums, however insisted that there was no room for worry. "The army was improving its performance and capabilities," he told Parliament in July 1962. He was proud of the extent of road building especially in the eastern sector which was more defensible. In August 1961, he declared in Parliament that "over the previous two years the balance of power had been changing in India's favour." On that subject, Nehru received regular pleasing information from the Minister of Defence Krishna Menon and also from the Chief of General Staff (CGS) Lieutenant General Kaul, a distant relative of Nehru. He rejected any criticism of the Indian soldier's equipment and decided that even though it did not reach the level of that of NATO soldier, it definitely fulfilled requirements.

Nehru was especially pleased with the growth in the logistic capabilities of the Indian air force. In October 1960, ten helicopters, 24 IL-14 cargo planes and eight AN-12 cargo planes were purchased. In 1961 another 13 Bell Helicopters were purchased. At the beginning of 1962 eight additional AN-12 and 16 MI-4 helicopters were ordered despite the dissatisfaction of the air force with the performance of the Soviet helicopters in the Himalayan heights (17,000 feet). In June 1962, 29 American Fairchild cargo planes were acquired and in 1962, in October, an agreement was signed with the USSR, in which the supply of two MIG squadrons and the establishment of an Indian aircraft industry to produce Soviet MIGs were promised.

His confidence in the ability of the Indian army, contrived by doctored reports, and his belief that the Chinese leadership would not take any extreme military steps against India, reinforced in his decision not to make concessions, and to go ahead with an active Forward Policy. The policy entailed patrolling and establishing positions in territory claimed by China as well as showing a presence and preventing a creeping take-over by Chinese forces of territory claimed as Indian. "This must be done," he told his aides "without getting involved in a clash with the Chinese, unless this becomes necessary in self-defence. Later, in October 1962, he even went so far as to instruct the army to evict Chinese forces that crossed the McMahon Line.

Various events reinforced Nehru's conviction that he had assessed the situation correctly. The Indian army's success in taking over Goa, in which he had challenged a US ally and a 'power' like Portugal and which action had not provoked the US and NATO, was proof of its efficiency. And thus India's well-established status in the international arena protected, Nehru thought, from the danger of massive retaliation from the Chinese.

Further this misperception was bolstered by a number of bilateral confrontations in which Chinese forces retreated or did not retaliate, the most prominent of them being in July 1962 in the Galwan Valley in the western sector. The Chinese army in Galwan Valley had surrounded an Indian position but retreated when the Indian forces stood firm threatening to retaliate against other Chinese positions in the western sector. This policy seemed to be successful as a calculated risk, or as Nehru put it in parliament: "We have taken the risk and we have moved forward, and we have stopped effectively their further march." The reliability of the deterrent effectiveness of the army and China's political and military weakness seemed thus proven.

In Nehru's view, the Forward Policy was "defensive." It was designed, Nehru stated, instead to contl in Chinese territorial "expansionism", based on the belief that if the Chinese could establish posts in the disputed territory, so could India.

India's Forward Policy nevertheless did have an offensive component since Indian troops were ordered to establish new "forward posts" in deep and remote areas of North-east Kashmir and in Arunachal Pradesh, even in those areas where the Chinese had already established their posts. By the autumn of 1962, the Forward Policy had become offensives to the point where India toyed with the possibility of evicting the Chinese from the Dhola-Thagla area.

The success of the Forward Policy, however, was dependent on China's refraining from open warfare. Unfortunately on this, Nehru had miscalculated and misjudged China.

In the summer of 1962 India's Forward Policy took on a new dimension ... Indian troops in April 1962 began establishing new check posts even in those areas that had been vacated by Chinese during the winter, and had not yet returned because snow had not melted. Indian troops and paramilitary forces began infiltrating behind Chinese check points in Ladakh. By the end of July, India had thus recovered control of about 5,000 square kilometres of territory in the Ladakh area that Nehru had cartographically laid claim to by publishing new maps.

In the NEFA area, the Indian government in February 1962 had decided to set up as many posts as possible along the McMahon Line; one of the new ones was Dhola in the Thagla area. This check-post was provocative for two reasons. First, the Dhola post was located in an area where the Chinese had questioned the exact demarcation of the McMahon Line, and where India really could not lay a firm claim. Second, the Dhola post was located close the Chinese base and thus could symbolize a threat to the Chinese position in Tibet.

India's Forward Policy was thus being devised to excite direct provocation by China. The forward probes behind Chinese positions in Ladakh and NEFA areas was interpreted by China as a sign of India's determination to assert its territorial claims by force. India's forward moves in the summer of 1962, proved counterproductive since it enabled China to get notice and be ready for counter-offensive in October 1962.

China prepared for the war, while India walked into it. China's response first manifested in forceful warnings to India. In the summer of 1962, as India began implementing the Forward Policy's provocative offensive, Beijing warnings became shriller. China warned India that if it did not withdraw its "aggressive posts and stop the provocations, Chinese frontier guards would be compelled to act in self-defence.

In July 1962, Chinese troops surrounded an Indian check-post in the Galwan river valley, Ladakh, and an exchange of fire resulted. But, then suddenly, the Chinese troops withdrew, which led to a false sense of complacency in New Delhi that China was reluctant to fight. But in September 1962, the Chinese began a forceful push in the Dhola-Thagla area in NEFA, encircling a key Indian post at Dhola. The Indian troops were first ordered to stay firm. The next day, they were ordered "to make immediate preparations to move forward within 48 hours and deal with the Chinese." The Chinese saw it as an Indian decision to use force to evict them from the Dhola-Thagla area. This time China was not as conciliatory as in the 1959-61 period.

Prior to Zhou's visit to New Delhi in 1960, tension had also increased on the frontiers. Action on the Indian side as early as August 25, 1959 had already led to the final bloody clash at Longju.

After the second bloody border clash at Kongka Pass on October 20, 1959, Zhou wrote again to Nehru on November 7, reiterating his earlier suggestions for maintaining the status quo of the border. He further suggested that both sides should withdraw their armed forces 20-km from the Line of Actual Control (LAC). Zhou came to New Delhi to meet Nehru between April 19 and 25, 1960. This was followed by three rounds of official meetings that year. However, all those efforts were sterile. Nehru, by now on the defensive, asked Zhou to meet individually his hard-liner Cabinet colleagues. In an unprecedented move, Zhou called on the senior Ministers of the Nehru government to explain China's point of view but received a cold reception from all the Ministers he met.

From 1961 onwards, the Indian armed forces, taking advantage of the stoppage of patrolling on the Chinese side perhaps because of internal developments in China, set up a series of checkposts on the western section of the border. On June 20, 1962, Nehru stated in the Indian Parliament that India had set up some new patrolling checkposts, challenging Chinese checkposts. Nehru told Parliament that India's position had thus improved on the ground, and would become even better in the future.

The then Indian Defence Minister, V.K. Krishna Menon, openly declared in early June 1962 that India would use military means to settle the boundary question with China, unmindful of our defence preparedness and gross misreading of the Chinese capacities. Then on September 26, 1962, Nehru declared at a press conference at Lagos in Nigeria that India would deal with the Chinese "by using force."

In the face of increasing tension on the Sino-Indian border, the Chinese Foreign Ministry sent notes to the Indian Embassy in Beijing on August 4, September 13, and October 3, 1962, and proposed to the Indian Government that the two sides should meet immediately without precondition in order to ease tension. But all the proposals were rejected by India, now on a high horse of its 'Forward policy.'

On October 12, 1962, Nehru told die press at New Delhi's Palam airport before he left for Sri Lanka that he had already "ordered the armed forces to clear the Chinese from the NEFA." That declaration of Nehru's was seen as India's ultimatum to China. Confirming this, on October 14, Indian Defence Minister V.K. Krishna Menon told a meeting of Congress workers at Bangalore that the Government had come to a final decision to "drive out the Chinese." He declared that the Indian Army was determined to fight the Chinese to the last man India almost did !

On October 18, 1962, Mao Zedong said at an enlarged meeting of the Chinese Communist Party's Politbureau: "For many years, we have taken a number of measures to seek a peaceful resolution of the boundary issue but India rejected all of them. They intentionally provoked even more violent armed clashes. They are bullying others too much. Now that Nehru is determined to fight with us, we have no way out but to keep him company. However, our counter attack is only meant to serve a warning to Nehru and the Government of India that the boundary question cannot be resolved by military means" [Quoted by Lai Yingfeng: My Days as a Military Staff in Supreme Command, Beijing 1997]. In the meantime, in July 1962, China had secretly agreed to reopen the talks with USA at Warsaw, Poland.

In these talks China offered to soften its attitude towards Taiwan and to the US presence in Korea and Japan. President John Kennedy of US then proposed further secret talks for normalization of relations of US with China, which he however could not see through to fruition. His bete noire, Nixon did that in 1971. Nehru was obviously not aware of the 1962 secret talks between US and China.

Thus, inexorably, China and India went to a war, a limited one but of long term consequence, which consequence has even now yet to fully unwind. The war was clearly the logical outcome of the state of opaque diplomacy between the Prime Ministers of the two countries who hid from each other their respective real agendas. Both played a zero-sum game, which however China won in 1962.

III. *Was there a deeper purpose in the minds of the leadership of the two countries for not resolving the conflict by negotiation in the 1950?*

On October 20, 1962 along the entire Sino-Indian frontier, a full fledged border war was launched. China with two to three divisions, equipped with modern weapons fell upon the Indian troops human wave upon wave, in all three sectors of the border, but with the main thrust in the NEFA and Ladakh areas. Indian and Chinese versions differ regarding the issue of who precipitated the war. India was taken by surprise, and was not at all prepared for such a scale of war. China's rapid advance, supported by a well established line of supplies and communications, gave further credence to the thesis that

China was fully prepared, and had chosen its own moment to strike.

It was China that first launched the offensive, with infantry and artillery. India's retaliation to the Chinese offensive was weak, uncoordinated and poorly planned. It proved disastrous. Like nine-pins, post after Indian military post collapsed into Chinese hands. Almost everywhere Indian troops, wholly unprepared for mountain warfare, outnumbered and outsmarted, were demoralized. Within less than four weeks, China gained occupation of all the territory which it claimed in the Ladakh and NEFA areas, leaving Indian army in tatters.

On November 20, 1962, China halted its this remarkable advance and declared a unilateral cease-fire. In the history of the modern world China may be the only country to declare a unilateral cease-fire, especially after such a rapid and substantial advance into foreign territory. And equally unprecedented, soon thereafter, China vacated the occupied territories and returned to their original position before the conflict. China, however warned of a return, if Indian forces attempted to re-occupy the vacated areas. The question remains: why China withdrew after such a successful advance? It clearly points to the possibility that having shown the world that China was not down and out after the events inside China of 1959-61, and having achieved its political aim of humbling India in the eyes of non-aligned and third world countries, it had no use for territories it could not defend when the snows would fall on the Himalayas in the bitter winter.

The Xinhua reported on May 26, 1963, that "the Chinese side had handed over to India all the 3,942 Indian military personnel captured during the Sino-Indian border conflict in

October and November 1962 as well as the bodies and ashes of 26 captured Indian military personnel who died."

On the occasion of the anniversary of the cease-fire, the People's Daily on November 21, 1963, carried an editorial announcing that the Chinese government was still awaiting negotiations with the Indian government on the border issue. It stated: "As far as China is concerned, the door is wide open for reopening Sino-Indian negotiations and for a peaceful settlement of the boundary question. China has patience. If it is not possible to open negotiations this year, we will wait until next year; if it is not possible next year, then the year after next."

The most plausible reason for the dramatic de-induction of Chinese military after November 20, 1962, and the subsequent offer of talks seems to be that China, having obtained military objectives, saw no further advantage in continuing the offensive. A further advance into the plains of India would have compromised the China's military position because its supply lines through the high and snowy mountains would have become indefensible, while India could have recovered from shock to deploy its conventionally trained army to better advantage, and perhaps deploy its relative superiority in airforce.

It is a mystery why in 1962 India did not stake its advantage in the air theatre. It can only be attributed to Nehru's loss of nerve, and reaping the consequences of Krishna Menon's encouragement of sycophancy in army promotions. His chosen commanders like B.K. Kaul had fled the battlefield pleading a "cold"! Other reasons for Chinese dc-induction could have been the anger and unity displayed by the Indian people against China, the fear of United States' intervention, and the risk of Russia's open support to India.

Thus, the strategic disadvantages of a continued war over the Himalayan mountains during the winter and the lack of any advantage in expanding its limited territorial claims in India, combined to convince China to stop her advance and declare the unilateral cease-fire. Nehru's reputation as a world leader was in shambles, and China may be have also been smug with the psychic satisfaction that the Tibetans wanting Independence could not hope anymore that India's military could liberate Tibet for a long time to come.

The Sino-Indian war of 1962 however was not simply an outcome of a border dispute. It emerged fundamentally from the problem of Tibet. China had liberated Tibet by force in 1950, and later had put down the rebellion in 1959. But the possibility of India providing the psychological syndrome for the Tibetan rebels to continue their struggle loomed large after the Dalai Lama had been given political asylum with great fanfare in India. But to a significant extent too, the 1962 offensive can be attributed to the Sino-Soviet dispute. China seemed to have believed that a strike against India would test that country's friendship with Soviet Union, expose thus the 'ideological error' of revisionist USSR's sup-port to "bourgeoisie" India, and thus emerge as the true adherent to communism.

## SINO-SOVIET DISPUTE AND INDIA

In September 1959, the TASS, the official news agency, had put out a statement on the August 1959 Longju incident referred to above. TASS. advised India and China to resolve the border conflict by "peaceful means." This equation of a socialist state (China) with a bourgeoisie one (India) by another socialist state (USSR), and implied equivocation on the issue enraged the Chinese leadership. On September 13,

1959, the Central Committee of the Chinese Communist Party (CCP) in a stiff letter to its counterpart in the Soviet Union (CPSU), accused the latter of "exposing the family secret" of the Sino-Soviet rift on the border dispute of China with India and thus betraying the Communist cause, that brought glee and jubilation among the Indian bourgeoise" (see Ranganathan and Khanna [27, pp. 15-16]).

It was not only the TASS reaction to the Longju incident that triggered the Chinese ire. Ever since the 'paternal' CPSU started demanding proof of acceptance of junior partner status by the CCP (e.g., by agreeing to place Chinese naval ports under Soviet supervision), the Soviet refusal to hand over a sample atom bomb and technical data since China "did not need the bomb," etc., the Chinese began to suspect that the Soviet Union might in the future collaborate with China's enemies such as USA and India to cap China's growth.

In a draft Report dated December 18, 1959 to the CPSU, Politburo's V. Suslov, the leading member responsible for CPSU's relations with foreign political parties, berated the CCP leadership for the edit page article in the official news daily, Renmin Ribao [People Daily] in May 1959, titled "The Revolution in Tibet and Nehru's Philosophy." Suslov commented that "Nehru had behaved with reserve on the Tibet issue, and that the present foreign policy line of the Nehru government is a positive factor in the struggle for strengthening peace." The term "present foreign policy" meant Nehru's non-alignment policy with a pro-Soviet tilt. Nehru acquiescence in the 1956 brutal crushing by the Soviet tanks of the Hungarian revolt had warmed the Soviet hearts. Suslov also ridiculed the view expressed by Chinese interlocutors that there was a possibility of a downfall of the Nehru government.

The Left-led massive Central Government employees strike in India in 1960 may have made the Chinese think that way, unable to comprehend bourgeoisie democracy and India's "functioning anarchy," as also then were possibly misled by Indian communists typical linguistic Marxist hyperbole on the imminent collapse of capitalism in India.

Subsequent events such as the withdrawal of Soviet technicians from China, stepping up Soviet assistance to India's Third Five Year Plan, the patronizing attitude of the CPSU towards the CCP after the failure of the Great Leap Forward, the Camp David summit of Khruschev with Eisenhower, convinced the Chinese that a grand alliance against China was emerging, consisting of the US, USSR and India.

Thus the Renmin Ribao [Peoples Daily] editorial opined on October 27, 1962, a week into the border war that "Nehru had become a pawn in the international anti-Chinese campaign. This is the root cause and background of the Sino-Indian boundary dispute."

Caught in the middle of the Cuban crisis then, the Soviet Union initially propitiated the Chinese by making statements supporting China against India. Indeed, the MIG 21 aircraft deal of August 1962 with India was suspended. USSR declared that Chinese were their "brothers" while Indians were merely a "friend."

But as soon as the Cuban crisis was over, the Soviet Union reverted back to neutrality on the Sino-Indian dispute. In December 1962, Nikita Khrushchev's address to the Soviet Parliament made that clear. Pravda, the official organ of the Soviet Communist Party in a major shift reflecting the Sino-Soviet growing rift wrote in their editorial of September 19,

1963: "... It is significant that, although the People's Republic of China Government strives to put all the blame for the conflict on the Indian Government, the non-aligned Afro-Asian nations deemed it necessary to urge none other than the Chinese Government to withdraw its forces twenty kilometres from the line which they reached as a result of major military operations in the autumn of 1962.... However, the Government of P.R.C. did not avail itself of the good services of these countries when they were offered.... No wonder, many people now say that the P.R.C. Government, while extolling in every way the initiative of the non-aligned nations, and declaring that it 'values' and 'pays tributes' to their good services, actually ignores these efforts and does not display any desire to profit by the proposals."

Years later in 1997, the Chinese officials permitted the publication of an interesting memoir [My Days as Military Staff in the Supreme Command, Jiangxi Province Government Publishing House, Chinese language edition, 1997] of General Lai Yingfeng, the commander of forces on the Tibet plateau during the late 1950s and in particular in 1962. General Lai wrote that Chairman Mao had summoned him, and he had called on him on October 10, 1962 ten days before the major assault by China across the Himalayas.

To Chairman Mao's almost rhetorical query as to why Nehru had wanted an armed conflict with China, General Lai had advanced three reasons which found favour with Mao: *First*, China, thought Nehru, was so weak that it was in no position to respond in distant south-west; *Second*, China was surrounded by USA and USSR on all sides and could not afford to take them on in a Sino-Indian military conflict; *Third*, the logistics of moving troops was so difficult for China that

Nehru thought that China could not deploy regular PLA troops to fight the Indian army.

According to General Lai, Chairman Mao then convened an extraordinary meeting of the politburo of CCP on October 18, 1962 wherein Gen. Lai presented his plans for armed deployment and engagement. Premier Zhou Enlai strongly advocated "counter attack in defence," positioning himself typically after sensing the mood—as hawk.

In his valedictory remarks, Chairman Mao concluded:

"Perhaps we may not win.... The worst result may be that India will occupy Tibet. But Tibet is China's sacred territory, everyone in the world knows this ... this can never change. We will someday recover it."

Years later in April 1981, Chairman Deng Xiaoping (who was a participant in the October 18, 1962 Politburo meeting) told me in Beijing that:

"There is the whole Tibetan plateau between us. There is very little oxygen and it is not even possible to deploy a large number of troops. Even if you were to take part of Tibet, therefore it would not be a threat to China. The real threat to us is from the North." [see Appendix II].

It was Tibet thus that is the bottom line in the Sino-Indian border dispute. In conclusion, hence, the deeper purpose of the border war was for China to expose to the world as vapid unrealistic view that India was in a position to intervene military in Tibet—to liberate it—prospect that Dalai Lama and 100,000 Tibetan abroad were propagating.

Besides this, China launched its offensive also to explode the myth of Nehru as a "world statesman" supported by the USA and USSR and hence unassailable. The Border claims were made the convenient excuse by China for achieving these deeper goals, which China did achieve in full measure by the decisive defeat of India on the ground in 1962.

The Chinese may have been offensive to Indian sentiments by stating that they "taught India a lesson in 1962," a refrain repeated by Deng Xiaoping in 1979 when China invaded Vietnam. But in every defeat there are lessons to be learnt which regrettably even today India has not learnt. Those who do not learn from history are condemned to relive it. The ostrich like approach to own up our follies and rectify it is the refusal of the Government to declassify the commissioned Henderson-Brookes Report of the 1962 truths. As Defence Minister, Parrikar has agreed to declassify it , but the remnant Nehru family toadies in government still managed to block it.

Nevertheless, the core truth on the Sino-Indian border dispute however remains evident even today: that is, neither the Indians nor the Chinese have an uncontestable case on the entire Border. The Chinese however have accepted the legitimacy of the Macmahon Line to demarcate the China-Myanmar international boundary in 1963. There is therefore no way the Chinese can deny India that Arunachal Pradesh-Tibet international boundary is the Indian claimed Macmahon Line. Chairman Deng in his 1981 one to one discussion with me put the matter this way: India keep Arunachal and recognize Chinese claims in Aksai Chin as a border solution.

I would it put it differently as an approach to the Border issue: China is has already committed to the Macmahon line as legitimate by signing a treaty with Myanmar recognizing the line. Hence it is not a concession to India under international law, but an admitted fact.

Therefore by conceding that legitimacy of the Indian claim that Macmahon line is the admitted border of Arunachal,

China would set the stage for a friendly negotiation with India on Aksai China, where India could make concessions on the Aksai Chin claims in the interest of China's appropriate security needs.

Therefore it is pragmatic on this basis for geographers and military experts of both countries to confabulate together and thrash out a mutually convenient and maintainable border.

It took 38 years, from 1950 to 1988, for the Government of India [during Prime Minister Rajiv Gandhi's China visit] to acknowledge that the Sino-Indian Border was indeed "disputed and undemarcated," and to be settled by negotiations. Now it is time to fast track it.

The national cost paid in strategic terms for the late recognition has been high: besides the human lives lost, it is the formation of a Sino-Pakistan axis, which did materially not exist before 1962, and which came into existence because of events leading upto this border war which was the real cost of the Sino-Indian conflict and which now poses the most formidable challenge to India's national security. And this burden is Nehru's folly and lasting legacy to India.

How now to unhinge thus and dismember the Sino-Pakistan compact is now the foremost strategic objective for India. For the Indian blood to flow at the will of Pakistan and its terrorist hordes, someday it has to pay price imposed by India such as its disintegration into four different countries Baluchistan, Pakhtoonistan, Sindh and residual Punjabi Pakistan.

Recent developments in Sino-Indian relations (1998-2018) however show that Indian leadership had yet to shake off that Nehru legacy of swinging from capitulation to irrational aggression.

What is required today is for India to first shed off all remnants of the old British imperialist inspired policy and concepts on Tibet [as detailed in Chapter 2], and then press for the most advantageous settlement of the Sino-Indian border (which could include Chinese recognition of the McMahon Line with a different nomenclature, as with Burma). Thereby, the groundwork would be laid to explore a future strategic partnership with China.

Before exploring whether there exists a negotiated solution to the Sino-Indian border dispute, a question which must be faced is the 1962 Indian Parliament resolution pledging the recovery of "lost territories". Legally, it can be argued that a Resolution does not survive a session of the Lok Sabha that had passed it. However, the really appropriate question is what Parliament and the people would consider today as "lost territories." With some education, there is reason to believe that a settlement broadly on the lines we shall suggest here would be received with satisfaction by the majority of the Indian people.

This would depend of course on the trade-offs that India works out with China. A settlement as a fresh determination of the border made jointly on agreed principles would be much better than one seen to result from "concessions", and "adjustments" by one side or the other.

The long-term relationship with China however is subject to several imponderables. If China seeks super power status and with a veto in Asian affairs, then India will face fresh problems. However, a settled border and relations normalised in the meantime, would allow India to face that eventuality with greater preparedness. Alternatively, India can become a partner with China in international initiatives, as well as in information technology and in cultural propagation. It is incumbent on Indian leadership to make a determined effort to investigate these possibilities.

However, in view of the fact that China has accepted in a treaty with Mynmar (Burma), the same MacMahon Line extended beyond India borders to Mynmar as the formal international border between China and Mynamar, therefore India is not required to negotiate with China to accept any modification on the Arunachal border with China, since it is part of the same MacMahon Line. The Ladakh – Xinjiang border would be however negotiated on the secure maintainability of the border by either side, China or India. But this must follow, not precede a Suno-Indian international understanding and strategic partnership.

# CHAPTER 3

# The Strategic Perspectives in Sino-Indian Relations

In retrospect, briefly then Sino-Indian relations in the past seven decades may be viewed in phases as follows:

### PHASE I: SINO-INDIAN FRIENDSHIP (1950-1958)

India was the first non-socialist country to establish formal diplomatic relations with the People's Republic of China. India was in the forefront in advocating that the People's Republic of China be recognized as the real China in the United Nations Security Council, and until 1962, voted for it in the UN (see Appendix IV).

With the signing of the Agreement between the People's Republic of China and the Republic of India on Trade and Intercourse between Tibet region of China and India and an Exchange of Notes in April 1954. India signed away all its inherited privileges in Tibet by virtue of earlier pacts. The Five Principles of Peaceful Co-existence (Panchsheel) in the preamble of the agreement, laid down the foundation for the development of friendship and cooperation between China and India.

In April 1955, the successful cooperation between China and India reached its peak at the Bandung Conference in Indonesia. It also set a high mark in Afro-Asian solidarity for independence from colonial rule.

## PHASE II: BOUNDARY DISPUTE AND TENSION IN RELATIONS (1959-4961)

Prime Minister Nehru expressed sympathy for the 1959 Tibet rebellion, and on more than one occasion stated that China enjoyed only 'suzerainty' over Tibet after agreeing to Chinese sovereignty, formalized in the 1954 Treaty. An "exile government" under the Dalai Lama became active in India although the Government of India had assured China that the Dalai Lama was in India only as a religious leader.

On January 23, 1959, Chinese Premier Zhou declared in a letter to Nehru that the boundary is disputed, shocking the latter. Prime Minister Nehru refused to negotiate a settlement, insisting that there was no boundary question at all, that the "McMahon line" was the legal boundary line in the eastern sector. In 1961-62, the India carried out the so-called "forward policy" with an aggressive content to rid of the Chinese "aggression," using force "if necessary." It was this "forward policy" that finally provoked China into armed intervention. The Sino-Indian trade agreement had expired at the end of 1959 but was not renewed.

## PHASE III: BORDER WAR AND ABNORMAL BILATERAL RELATIONS (1962-1976)

Border war broke out on October 27, 1962, and ended on November 7, 1962. In December 1962, India withdrew its consulates-general from Lhasa and Shanghai forcing the Chinese to close down Calcutta and Mumbai consulates, on India's demand. The Xinhua News Agency correspondent was ordered to leave India, China publications were banned in India, the properties of the Bank of China's branch offices in

Calcutta and Bombay were taken away by the Indian authorities and overseas Chinese were detained in prison. Sino-Indian bilateral relations thus came down to its nadir.

Sino-Indian relations remained abnormal for 15 long years (1961-1976), although India's Foreign Secretary put out the first diplomatic feeler on November 12, 1969, for sending back India's Ambassador to Beijing. The new Ambassador, however, actually arrived in Beijing only in July 1976. The Indian government took six years and eight months to put this decision into action. Soviet Union's pressure had delayed the process.

### PHASE IV: SLOW NORMALIZATION PROCESS (1977-1988)

In 1978, the Janata Party initiated serious political initiatives to befriend China, despite dire warning from Soviet Premier Alexei Kosygin, broadcast over Indian government controlled TV, the Doordarsban to the Indian people made on March 9, 1979. The high point of 1981 in April was the meeting of the this author, the then Janata Party Deputy Leader in Parliament Dr. Subramanian Swamy with China's Supremo Deng Xiaoping's for 100 minutes in a one to one discussion in the Great Hall of the People.

In that meeting, Chairman Deng told this author that at his request China would reopen the Kailash Manasarovar holy spot for Hindu pilgrim in batches and asked this author lead the first batch to the holy spot, which was gladly accepted. Chairman Deng also accepted his suggestion to send China's Foreign Minister to India to resume normal relations. Chairman Deng also accepted this author's suggestion that China oblige India, in that Assam agitating students seeking arms from China be arrested and handed over to the Indian Border Police.

That historic meeting began the thaw in relations. During this author's return from the walkathon to Kailash holy mountain and Manasarovar lake, a grateful Prime Minister, Indira Gandhi sent me an Airforce helicopter to pick the author up while returning back from via Lipu Lekh Peak at Kalapani Air force base there, a helicopter sent picked the author. From late 1981, China and India started regular dialogue at the level of Vice-Foreign Minister. An impasse however developed due to Soviet Union's concern at the developing relations which was effective at slowing the improvement till 1988. Other hangovers from 1962 also remained due to frozen minds. In 1986, for example, the then Minister of State for Personnel, P. Chidambaram, told Parliament that the ban on Chinese publications and its import into India would not be rescinded since these publications supported "class struggle and other seditious Marxist ideas" probably due to Soviet Union's influence.

## PHASE V: IMPASSE BROKEN: INITIATIVES IMPROVE RELATIONS (1988-1998)

Prime Minister Rajiv Gandhi's visit to Beijing from December 19 to 23, 1988, broke the impasse by acknowledging a "disputed boundary" on the frontiers. For about a decade thereafter, Sino-Indian bilateral relations developed steadily and smoothly. The ban on Chinese publications was lifted. Prime Minister P.V. Narasimha Rao visited China in 1993 and President Jiang Zemin visited India in 1996 and laid the institutional foundation for the relations to progress through two important Confidence Building Measure (CBM) Agreements of Maintenance of Peace and Tranquillity in the Border Areas along the Line of Control (LAC). The turnover of the bilateral trade which was a mere $246 million in 1988, increased to more than $2 billion in 1998.

## PHASE VI: SHARP DETERIORATION IN RELATIONS (MAY 1998 TO DATE)

On May 11, 1998, India conducted underground nuclear tests in the desert of Rajasthan. The next day, Prime Minister A.B. Vajpayee wrote a secret letter to the heads of G-8 nations, accusing China of posing nuclear threat to India and having committed "armed aggression" against India in 1962, undoing a decade of confidence building. Indian Defence Minister George Fernandes publicly referred to China as "the number one potential threat" to India. Sino-Indian relations sank to a new low.

A year later External Affairs Minister Jaswant Singh came to Beijing (in June 1999) for talks with his Chinese counterpart. Chinese Foreign Minister Tang Jiaxuan pointed out that the prerequisites for the development of Sino-Indian relations should be that neither side should see the other as a threat and that the Five Principles of Peaceful Co-existence should be taken as the basis. And although meekly Jaswant Singh agreed, the relations did not progress. Disconcerting indications of tense relations became increasingly apparent. Chinese reversed the earlier conciliatory stands on the border negotiations and the Kashmir issue, and issued sharp statements.

Noted writer on strategic affairs, and critique of the developing Sino-Indian relations, Brahma Chellaney, wrote in 'The Hindustan Times,' news daily (January 31, 2000 edition) that Jiang Zemin, the Chinese supremo, made some highly derogatory references to India in a meeting with the head of state "of one of the world's major powers."

The scorn Jiang poured on India and the warning he delivered were extraordinary. This report was not been denied. Chellaney opined that for India, Jiang's comments were a reminder that "without a clearheaded. long-term China policy, it risks further trouble." Jiang reportedly told the head of state that he had decided to test India's defence preparedness by sending Chinese military patrols across the line of actual control (LAC). This happened both in Ladakh while the 1999 Kargil war was raging and later along the Arunachal Pradesh frontier as well.

For this Jiang had summoned chief executives of the two provinces adjoining India, to Beijing and discussed India's military alertness and response capability. Quoting Jiang, Chellaney reported: "Each time we tested them by sending patrols across, the Indian soldiers reacted by putting their hands up," Jiang had said mockingly. Chinese military patrols had sporadically challenged the Indian Army in Ladakh while Pakistan was waging war in Ladakh's Kargil-Dras sectors in May-July 1999. Later, the Chinese built up tensions at the other end of the border with India in Arunachal through aggressive military manuevers in the Tawang sector in September 1999. Obviously the wounds of 1962 had not healed on either side.

In 1962, the issue was the Tibetan revolt in March 1959, and India's subsequent ill prepared aggressive posturing that had led to the outbreak of hostilities. The Chinese suppression of the Tibetan revolt was portrayed by India as violation of Tibetan autonomy, thus a violation of the 1951 Sino-Indian Agreement on Tibet. Beijing was then dismayed by India's reactions to the Tibetan situation, the granting of political asylum to the Dalai Lama and 35 others in his entourage, as well as to create a Lhasa-type town in Dharmshala in Himachal Pradesh near the Tibet border where a Tibet "Exile" Government was put in place; the help to the Tibetan rebels in Kalimpong, but most irritating to the Chinese was India's guarded but vocal concern about Tibetan independence.

India had become home to 100,000 Tibetan refugees as well. China, in a preemptive action to protect its hold on Tibet, began in August 1959 to push ahead in Aksai Chin area. The conflict in Longju and Kongka Pass, causing casualties signaled China's new frontier policy which the Nehru government should taken seriously but did not.

In response to China's "frontier policy," India developed a counter-move to convert aggressively the "forward policy" initiated since 1954, but which was since then sporadically implemented. A fresh Government Directive in November 1961 to the Indian Army HQ, was passed on to Area Commanders on December 5, 1961.

The Forward Policy was designed to contain China's further advance, establish India's presence in Ladakh, to be in a position to cut Chinese supply lines, and ultimately to force a withdrawal. Nehru, however misperceived that the Chinese would not respond, which was perhaps in his seventeen year tenure as Prime Minister his greatest folly. The policy was obviously based on the false premise that the Chinese would not risk an open war with India or use force against Indian posts in Ladakh and NEFA areas.

China's domestic problems may also have been another motivating factor in the military move in the Ladakh and NEFA areas. The failure of the so-called "Great Leap Forward" in 1959, and the change of leadership in the Communist Party in 1958-59, created an impression internationally that China had become weak, and incapable of resisting nibbling on its borders. India was also preening on its victory in Goa in December 1961 over a rag-tag Portuguese occupation force.

Nehru began openly speaking about use of force "if necessary to clear Indian territory of Chinese 'incursions' swayed perhaps by military victory in Goa and encouraged by NATO's non-response to Goa's military takeover despite Portugal being a member of that US-led military alliance.

The events of autumn 1959, such as the localized military conflict in the Ladakh and NEFA areas, and China's now public substantial territorial claims, had evoked a belligerent response from the Indian Parliament and the people as well. Nehru broke the news of the border dispute to Parliament in September, 1959 when he submitted White Paper Number One on Sino-Indian relations.

This was the first time that the public had been informed by its government about a border dispute which had been in existence since 1954, while Indian people were made to chant 'Indians and Chinese are brothers'. The White Paper came thus as a "big surprise" to the Indian Parliament and the public.

A clamour grew for effective rebuttal, especially by opposition parties and even from some influential members of Congress such as Mahavir Tyagi, MP, who later even demanded Nehru's resignation if he would not sack Defence Minister Krishna Menon. Nehru did finally sack Menon in 1962, after the October defeat.

China, in the summer of 1961 had begun a new push into the NEFA areas, started patrolling along the McMahon Line, began establishing new posts, and reached the Dhola-Thagla area, where India in June earlier, had already set up a new post.

In pursuance of its policy, the Chinese by September 1962 had occupied almost 19,000 square kms of territory in Ladakh and had penetrated along the south of the McMahon Line as far as they could, upto stationed Indian troops in the NEFA area.

There is also a view with some circulation, that the Chinese unable to understand India's 'functioning anarchy', decided to put pressures as a part of a long range plan for derailing India's "bourgeoisie" democracy in favour of the Communists' concept of "People's Democracy." But there is no evidence to sustain this view the China sought Balkanisation of India, since from 1959 to 1963, China had settled border disputes with Burma, Nepal and Pakistan, without furthering "People's Democracy" in these countries of even greater affliction of anarchy than India then. And would China have liked the emergence of another giant Communist neighbour, India, especially since by then the Sino-Soviet rift was known to both?

Moreover, the Kuomintang's nationalists, placed in the same military position, would have done the same thing the Chinese communists did in Tibet. And throughout the second half of the 20th century, Taiwan had taken a similar stand on the Sino-Indian border problem as the Communists. The claims over Tibet, as well as the boundary claims in the Himalayan region, are viewed by the Chinese on both sides of the Taiwan Straits as legitimate goals of Chinese nationalism, and thus which has little to do with ideological motivation.

It is my considered view that, instead, an important motivating factor for Chinese military response to India in 1962 was the Sino-Soviet dispute. This view, with much evidentiary support has now been articulated by many astute observers. The growing friendly relations between the USSR and India since 1955, and substantial Soviet economic and military aid to India, against the expressed opposition of China, motivated Beijing to put military pressure on India to test Soviet friendship with India, and to embarrass the Russians for having withdrawn Soviet experts and blue prints from China in 1960.

The Chinese probably also wanted the Russians [who had re-fused to discuss border disputes then with China] to know that China was ready to use its military power to sustain its territorial claims. That is, while the Indian ambivalence on Tibet and seemingly tacit support to rebels was the incendiary factor, it was the growing Sino-Soviet dispute of the 1950s which was the trigger for the 1962 conflict.

## SINO-PAKISTAN FRIENDSHIP

Sino-Pakistan nexus in military strategy and tactics have a significant bearing on India's environment. This nexus has remained remarkably stable over the last four decades, and which has remained ideologically neutral and immune to tumultuous changes in international relations. But what must be remembered is that China did not intervene in any of the last three India-Pakistan Wars – 1965, 1971, or 1999.

When Pakistan joined SEATO in 1954 and CENTO in 1955, military alliances which were established to contain communist influence, China surprisingly did not object. Prime Minister Zhou Enlai in fact, took the extraordinary step to explain to the Afro-Asian Conference in Bandung [in April 1955] that "the Prime Minister of Pakistan told me that although Pakistan was party to a military treaty, Pakistan was not against China. Pakistan had no fear that China would commit aggression against her. As a result of that, we achieve a mutual understanding, although we are still against military treaties." The Prime Minister of Pakistan even reiterated that in the event of a global war launched by the USA against China, Pakistan would not be a party to it. Zhou Enlai told the Associated Press of Pakistan on April 10, 1963 that because of "certain Pakistan assurances since 1954 on-wards, China "approved" of Pakistan's objectives of acquiring political and military superiority over India in joining SEATO and CENTO, since otherwise "Pakistan had no other motivation in joining the pacts." Pakistan had joined these pacts, according to Premier Zhou, for "defensive" reasons, and therefore it would not adversely affect overall Sino-Pak relations.

In 1956, China had made its first pronouncement, in a India-related dispute [despite the Panchsheel Declaration of 1954], when in talks with a Pakistani Press delegation in Beijing, Zhou Enlai said: "China accepted the existence of Kashmir dispute and hoped that it would be settled peacefully."

In January 1961, China entered into negotiations with Pakistan for the demarcation of the border (in Pakistan-occupied Kashmir]. In May 1962, the two governments recognised the need to "locate and align their common border" and expressed their wish to demarcate the boundary between China's Sinkiang province and the contiguous areas "the defence of which is under the actual control of Pakistan." The statement said that the agreement would be of a "provisional nature," and that China would renegotiate with the "sovereign authority" after the settlement of the dispute over Kashmir between India and Pakistan. India's strong protest fell on deaf ears.

On December 27, 1962 a month after the Sino-Indian border war was over, a joint Sino-Pak communique clearly expressed that "an agreement in principle has been reached on the location and alignment of the boundary actually existing between the two countries." The Sino-Pak bound-ary agreement was effective from March 2, 1963, under which Pakistan ceded to China 3,200 square kms of Kashmir territory to China. Foreign Minister Zulfiqar Bhutto in July 1963 told Pakistan's National Assembly that Pakistan could now rely on Chinese support in the event of an Indo-Pak war. Obviously, China had decided to make Pakistan a strategic ally, for which the latter was willing to pay a price.

From 1966 to 1968, Pakistan acquired 100 T-9 (Soviet variant) tanks, 80 MIG-19s (F-6) and 10 llyushin-28 bombers. This substantially made up for the losses during the 1965 war with India over Kashmir. Since then, China has been one of Pakistan's main suppliers of military equipment. Arms transfers from China to Pakistan from 1966 to 2000 amounted to more than an estimated $6.00 billion. Military supplies were given free of cost till 1978, and since then at cost price.

There has been considerable nuclear collaboration between the China and Pakistan since 1965) with North Korea fitting in the gaps. The degree of Chinese participation in Pakistan's nuclear programme is an indication of the degree of its commitment in Pakistan's security. Beijing has been a constant supplier of a variety of nuclear products and services to Pakistan, ranging from uranium enrichment technology to research and power reactors, although China claims that these meet IAE standards.

In September 2000 a study published by the Centre for Non-Proliferation Studies at the Monterey Institute of International Studies in USA, has details about how China helped Pakistan become a significant nuclear and missile power in South Asia.

The study had concluded as early as 1983, that Beijing had by then transferred a complete nuclear weapon design to Islamabad, along with enough weapons-grade uranium for two nuclear weapons. In 1986, China concluded a comprehensive nuclear cooperation agreement with Pakistan and in the same year, it began assisting Islamabad with the enrichment of weapons-grade uranium. China also reportedly transferred enough tritium gas to Pakistan for 10 nuclear weapons.

In 1989, China, the study claimed, involved Pakistani scientists in a nuclear test at its Lop Nor test site. In 1994-95, China sold ring magnets to A.Q. Khan Research Laboratory at Kahuta which were used in gas centrifuges to make weapons-grade enriched uranium.

The destination of these magnets, to the research lab which is not subject to IAEA safeguards is believed used in Pakistan's nuclear weapons programme.

The credit for procuring Chinese nuclear technology for Pakistan goes to Bhutto's visit to Beijing in May 1976. Two crucial agreements emerged from it: (1) scientific cooperation in nuclear energy and (2) military cooperation. For the first time a joint China-Pakistan Military Committee was also established. In the nuclear field, China agreed to supply heavy water to Pakistan. There was to be cooperation between the two countries in plutonium reprocessing and collaboration on uranium enrichment through the centrifuge method. When the French government informed the Zia government in 1978 that it was unable to proceed with the Chashma deal unless Pakistan agreed to revise the original agreement providing for co-processing of spent fuel, the Chinese came to Pakistan's rescue.

On September 15, 1986, a formal agreement on cooperation in the nuclear field between Pakistan and China was signed during the visit of Pakistan's Prime Minister Junejo to Beijing. The agreement was for cooperation in the 'peaceful' uses of nuclear technology and has safeguards provisions against the proliferation of nuclear weapons in accordance with the ones laid down by the International Atomic Energy Agency.

China's nuclear weapon programme has reached the stage where its SLBM, the CSS-N-3, can be deployed aboard the nuclear-powered Xia-class submarines in large numbers. These missiles have a range of 2,800 km and can pose a threat to the Indian land mass; when these submarines start entering the waters of the Indian Ocean, India will face a potential threat. The Chinese nuclear submarines entering the Indian Ocean would need R&R and the Karachi has excellent port facilities for that purpose.

China now has about a 15-year lead over India in the nuclear field, after being behind India in 1958. Since Sino-Pak nuclear understanding against India is not an improbability in the future, therefore if India does not restructure its foreign policy suitably, it would become highly vulnerable to Pakistan's nuclear blackmail.

The Sino-Pak axis was strategically strengthened by the reopening in 1967 of the old silk route—the Karakoram Highway—which linked Chinese Xinjiang with Pak-occupied Hunza valley in Kashmir. This meant the opening of a direct route for supply of arms that would remain undisturbed in any future contingency. This supply route potentially poses a more serious threat to India's security than any quantum of armaments that Pakistan may receive. The safety of this particular Sino-Pak highway against possible attack has been guaranteed by the construction of a number of military bases all along the route. The Karakoram Highway linking Gilgit with Beijing was formally inaugurated in June 1978. These roads were demonstrations of China's firm commitment to consolidate and perpetuate its close ties with Pakistan. But the late Osama Bin Laden gang reached Xinjiang by this highway, which had perturbed China. This led to the formation of the Shanghai Five in which Pakistan has been denied entry. How far this development will mar Sino-Pakistan relations in future, is too early to speculate today.

Pakistan by itself however cannot never be a major threat to India's security. If China shares with Pakistan a common hostility towards India, only then India's security is seriously threatened by Pakistan. To nullify thus this, requires that Indian leadership be astute, and alert to any possibility of a rupture in Sino-Pakistan relations, and then to seize it when it obtains. This will test Indian political leadership's practical sense and street smartness in international affairs.

The 1962 war brought home the brutal fact that Nehru was not internationally savvy as Indians had thought. Nehru was gravely in error in his unrealistic assessment of China, about the geostrategic international environment, on the preparedness of the Indian army and on the balance of military power with China. Not to be in the same plight in the future, it is important hence that Indian leadership study China's strategy more seriously than hitherto. China cannot be taken for granted, because starting from Mao's declaration that: "China has stood up," China is well on its way to becoming a 'global economic and military power, second only to the United States of America.'

Strategically speaking, India has a long border with China (3,850 kms), a sizeable boundary with Pakistan, and an enormously long coast line. Indians have in the last five decades seen military action on *all three fronts:* In 1962, on the China-India border; in 1965, on the Pakistan border; and in 1971, on its coastal seas when a task force of the US Seventh Fleet streamed into the Bay of Bengal uninhibited and carrying nuclear weapons on board on one of its ships. According to one recent biography, the US President Richard Nixon in 1971 was inclined to use those nuclear weapons on India to prevent the total destruction of Pakistan, which was within the realm of possibilities on December 16, 1971, after the creation of Bangladesh by the Indian armed forces that obtained on the surrender of Pakistani occupation forces in Dacca on that day.

A Chinese direct intervention on behalf of Pakistan in 1965 and 1971, however did not occur for fortuitous but unforeseen reasons. In 1965, because China was on the verge of a domestic turmoil that led to the Cultural Revolution, in which the PLA became embroiled. China did nevertheless engage in some verbal brinkmanship. On September 16, 1965, an official note was sent by China to India which accused India of "setting up 56 posts on the Tibetan side of the Sikkim sector, kidnapping Tibetan civilians, and committing 300 infiltrations since 1962." China demanded dismantling of the so-called posts within 72 hours, and began amassing troops along the Sino-Indian border. It also demanded that India return a 1000 yaks that were allegedly stolen by India! But because of the aforementioned constraint, the Chinese did not act on their ultimatum, and on the day the UN-mediated ceasefire came into effect on September 22, China announced that India "had met the conditions." China nevertheless vehemently opposed the 1966 Tashkent conference as a Soviet conspiracy. Soon thereafter China began its military supplies to Pakistan to prevent a possible further improvement in Soviet relations with Pakistan.

Nevertheless, the 1965 Pakistani aggression against India was encouraged by the increasingly strong vocal support that Beijing had given to Pakistan's position on Kashmir, which made the Pakistani leaders believe that if it made a move against India, it would have strong Chinese military backing as well for its actions. A further provocation came when Zhou Enlai held talks in Algiers late 1964 with Sheikh Abdullah. Abdullah was arrested immediately on his return to India and remained in jail for a decade. Encouraged, Pakistan despatched 5,000 plus Islamic guerrillas to enter Kashmir. Soon followed the September 1965 war with India.

Chinese also did not intervene in the 1271 Bangladesh War on behalf of Pakistan of perhaps or possibly because of the September 1971 aborted coup attempt by Defence Minister Lin Biao. As a consequence of the failed attempt, Chairman Mao ordered all airforce planes to be grounded and the PLA demobilized. Hence, India was twice lucky by unrelated internal developments in China, which had prevented a joint China-Pakistan operation against India. But no nation can structure its strategic perceptions and options on the presumption of such luck obtaining every time.

Today, India needs to understand why it is important, strategically, to resolve the border dispute with China amicably and how to, by removing the deeper causes that fuel the Sino-Indian tensions, lay a secure foundation for future Sino-Indian relations. If India does so, she shall have learnt the real lessons of 1962. That is now of concern in this chapter. As we have seen above, India's relationship with the People's Republic of China over the past fifty years had traversed the entire spectrum: from the initial phase of amity and camaraderie, to outright hostility, followed by a protracted period of mutual suspicion and antagonism, then gradual thawing, but culminating at the end of the century into a phase of "uneasy co-existence."

In the 1990s while both sides were taking measured steps to narrow "their differences," India's nuclear tests of May 1998 and the accompanying justification by the Prime Minister of India to the US President, holding out the Chinese threat as the reason for the tests, rudely disrupted that process. The period since 1998 had seen a new phase of incremental hostility between India and China, which culminated through peaks and trough in the Bhutan 2017 face-off.

## THE FUNDAMENTAL PROBLEMS OF INDIA AND CHINA RELATIONS

A fundamental problem in Indian policy-making towards China is that there is no apparent consensus in India even today, on the "end" objectives of engagement with China. The domestic strategic discourse so far has also failed to come up with a clear criterion for evaluating the "means" to be adopted in this regard.

There is as yet no clear India's China perspective inside the Government. It is in this context that a review of contemporary Sino-Indian relations was undertaken in Chapters 1 and 2 in this Chapter therefore, we concern ourselves of the crucial national security imperatives that necessitate developing stable Sino-Indian relations. During the next two decades, India will need to make crucial choice: Whether to form a compact with China (Choice I) or become a part of the US efforts to keep China 'contained' (Choice II). How and why that choice is made is the subject of the analysis below.

India's tense security relationship with China following the 1962 border war underwent a qualitative change in the late 1980s and in the 1990s. The institutionalized bilateral interaction based on the Peace and Tranquility Agreement (PTA) of 1993, enabled the two sides to hold eight rounds of talks covering a wide range of issues. These have included clearer demarcation of the Line of Actual Control (LAC), no new troop deployments along the LAC, and a range of military-technical confidence building measures (CBMs) detailed at the command levels.

The two countries have agreed to maintain the LAC as the defacto boundary pending its negotiated settlement. In the meantime, the two have engaged in wider dialogue through the joint working groups, which last met in July 2000. However, despite the calm on the LAC front, serious issues of dispute have again emerged in the relations that could embitter the bilateral relations in the 21st century.

This requires elucidation and formulating a policy to normalize the situation. Either India befriends China in a fundamental and strategic sense, or India confronts China. There is no room for ct worthwhile third alternative option. To make the choice, India needs to be clear on its nuclear posture vis-a-vis China. The point requiring clarification is the content of India's nuclear doctrine. The government of India has stated that the doctrine envisages "no first use" of nuclear weapons and only seeks to establish a "survivable second strike capability." Once India is able to launch missiles from aboard ships or from submarines, the delivery options will significantly lend content to the otherwise vague concept of "second strike capability," a concept incidentally in disuse in the West.

Beijing has also committed to "no first use" and "non-use against non-nuclear powers." This, on the face of it, should end nuclear confrontation between China and India, if both sides are committed to that without ambiguity. Does, for example, China's "no first use" declaration prevent its use on its "own territory," or in the Sino-Indian context, in any of the 'disputed' territories, e.g., Arunachal or Aksai Chin? Thus, it is possible for China to launch a pre-emptive first strike, using tactical nuclear weapons against Indian counter force targets in a disputed region without violating the letter of declaration of 'no first use'. There is, of course, in 'addition the possibility that China could launch a massive nuclear first strike against strategic targets in India because India had launched a pre-emptive strike against Pakistan, or even in second strike using nuclear weapons against Pakistan. This, China could hold, is not "first use." Thus, there is Considerable area of ambiguity that would need to be cleared up in a Sino-Indian understanding. At the present state of relations, however, China would prefer that the ambiguity remain.

The Indian doctrine aims for a second strike capability that would survive a Chinese first strike and retaliate by inflicting unacceptable damage upon the adversary. Theoretically, in the strategic domain, this envisages second strike capacity to counter force targets and major counter value targets in the Chinese heartland. In the tactical domain, it envisages capacity to launch strikes against select counter force targets near the border. India would be in a position, according present Defence plans, to deploy the naval version of the Prithvi missile by 2005 and the Sagarika submarine-launched cruise missile by about 2010. Both of these missiles, capable of sea-skimming and radar-evading flight trajectories, would complement its land based deterrent options against China.

However, as the Indian government elaborates its nuclear doctrine, the paradigm of the "minimum deterrence" has to be visualized prudently, in qualitative and quantitative terms. For example, if India were to include reactor-grade fuel to fabricate nuclear weapons, the total nuclear stockpile required would be between 390 and 470 weapons, as compared to China's 450 weapons. Is India inclined to tread this expensive path? Without a credible Sino-Indian understanding, it would be inevitable. But the Indian government of today has proceeded in a rather abrasive manner with China on this issue.

On May 11-13, 1998, Prime Minister Vajpayee had made two announcements on the conduct of thermonuclear tests. Contrary to popular belie; the announcement did not disrupt the normalized Sino-Indian relations. In fact, the Chinese government official reaction was, although critical of India, not hostile or shrill. On May 12, 1998 the Chinese government spokesman merely stated that it was "seriously concerned," and that the tests were "detrimental to peace and stability in the South Asian region."

This was in sharp contrast to the language of the US reaction, which had accused India of "creating a dangerous new instability in the region," and that it was "a very, very negative development" (which reaction was accompanied by US action of imposing sanctions). Germany went even further, and called the tests "a slap in the face" of 149 countries which have signed the Comprehensive Test Ban Treaty (CTBT), and the NPT.

The sharp Chinese reactions however came. only after May 15, 1998, when it called the tests an "outrageous contempt of the common will of the international community" and that these "not only threatened china but other neighbours as well." Thereafter China had progressively hardened its stand, and had practically frozen any politically significant interaction with the Indian government.

And what happened between May 12 and May 15-18 that had so thoroughly shaken the Chinese and embittered them? A series of actions and words of the Vajpayee Government since it came to office on March 19, 1998, culminating in the letter written by the Prime Minister to US President Clinton (which was leaked by the US sources to the New York Times, May 13, 1998) had, according to my understanding convinced the Chinese leaders that the Indian government was laying the foundation for emerging as a "counter weight" to China, and to pursue policies that would seek to undermine China's security and integrity. The tone and content of Vajpayee's letter to Clinton, which was to be kept confidential indicated that the Indian Prime Minister wanted the US patronage to emerge as the counter weight. That is, China perceived that India had made Choice I.

In Vajpayee's letter to Clinton, there are clear references to the "threats" from China and Pakistan. If what happened in 1962, 1965 and 1971 with China and Pakistan constitute a continuing threat in 1998 as Vajpayee pointed out, then did not the US despatch of its Seventh Fleet task force led by aircraft carrier HISS Enterprise into the Bay of Bengal in the 1971 War with enough nuclear weapons board to wipe out India's civilization, constitute by the same logic a continuing threat from the US in 1998? This omission to the 1971 US role from Vajpayee's letter could not be treated as an oversight. It was obviously to placate the US. It reflected an unsolicited tilt, since otherwise the Clinton administration would not have chosen to leak the letter to the press.

It is not the intention here to discuss the reasons for India's decision to go nuclear or to comment on India's concerns regarding the "deteriorating security environment" in general, and the China factor in this regard in particular.

By sheer diplomatic insensitivity, Atal Behari Vajpayee's letter to Clinton cited China as the major reason for its nuclear explosions. Wrote Vajpayee: "... We have an overt nuclear weapons state on our borders, a state which committed armed aggression against India in 1962. Although our relationship with that country has improved in the last decade or so, an atmosphere of distrust persists mainly clue to the unresolved border problem. To add to the distrust, that country has materially helped another neighbour of ours to become a covert nuclear weapon state."

At one level, there is nothing startlingly new or revealing in this letter as regards the Indian position on China. These facts have appeared in the Annual Defence Reports brought out by the Indian Ministry of Defence. The Annual Report for 1996-97 at the height of the new bonhomie with China, for instance clearly spelt out "India's concerns regarding China's defence cooperation with Pakistan's clandestine nuclear-programme and the sale of missiles and sophisticated weapons systems by it to Pakistan," which concerns were "conveyed to the Chinese side." The Report also mentioned the "... progress that China has made in the recent years in upgrading her nuclear arsenal and missile capabilities (which) will continue to have relevance for India's security concerns.

Upgradation of China's logistic capabilities all along the India-China border for strengthened air operations has to be noted." Nor the problem is, as the Chinese mentioned in their official statement of May 14, 1998, that India "... maliciously accused China of posing a nuclear threat to India" and that this "gratuitous accusation" was "solely for the purpose of finding an excuse for the development of its nuclear weapons." The problem arose, instead because these were articulated by

Vajpayee not to the Indian Parliament, which was in session then, but to the US President in almost a supplicant fashion.

The Prime Minister, in his subsequent clarificatory statements to Parliament in September 1998, stressed the fundamental Indian desire to have friendly relations with China and a satisfactory solution to the border dispute through negotiation. Ile also emphasized that by working together, India and China would serve not only bilateral interests, but regional and global ones as well. In October, the Principal Secretary to Prime Minister Vajpayee, also stressed that India did not regard China as an enemy. However, till the end of 1998, none of these overtures mollified the Chinese. It was only after the Foreign Minister went to Beijing, and formally announced the "withdrawal" of the earlier statement of China-is-a-threat-to-India, that China relented to a scheduling of the JWG meeting, held in July 2000.

The tenth JWG meeting had taken place in New Delhi in August 1997. The eleventh JWG meeting was held on 26 April 1998, the two delegations being led by the Indian Foreign Secretary and the Chinese Vice Foreign Minister, respectively. However, examining the outcome of the India-China dialogue and interaction after the twelfth JWG meet in July 2000, it is apparent that there has been no forward movement at all in Sino-Indian relations. A chill prevails. The latent mistrust has deepened on both sides. Of late, the Chinese have begun referring to the UN Resolution on Kashmir in the context of solving that problem, another change yet from the position of neutrality that had been in evidence since 1991 and given shape during Jiang Zemin's 1996 visit to the subcontinent.

In September 2000, in a major shift of gears, China blamed India for the scant progress in Sino-Indian border talks.

Chinese Assistant Foreign Minister Wang Yi in an interview to a group of visiting Indian journalists (in Beijing, on September 10, 2000) said: "What is important is that the two sides should have the sincerity and show mutual accommodation instead of one-way accommodation."

In India's reckoning, China is in illegal possession of 43,180 sq. kms of Kashmir, which include 5,180 sq. kms ceded to China by Pakistan under the Sino-Pakistan Boundary Agreement of 1963. China on the other hand holds that Indian maps show some 90,000 sq. kms of Chinese territory, as India's. Furthermore, expounding China's stand on the Kashmir issue, Wang noted that the Kashmir issue has long become stalemated. "So I think, lie said, "the only way out is the peaceful settlement with the help from the international community."

Which indicates another change in Beijing's stand. China's official media, in a series of articles articulated this view holding that the Kashmir issue involved three parties: India, the Kashmiri people and Pakistan. All these facts demonstrate that Sino-Indian relations are still in a tinder box.

The inclusion of China and Pakistan in Vajpayee's letter to Clinton, and the omission in that letter of reference to the 1971 US nuclear threat [which according to a recent biography of Nixon, the then US President, was real and ominous], was seen by the Chinese, justifiably, as an attempt to curry favour with US and an oblique suggestion that India was ready to be considered as a counter weight to China.

The US did not however bite, and by leaking the letter to the New York Times, obviously with Clinton's approval, it showed up Vajpayee in very poor light. Of course, if India ultimately emerged as a counter weight to China by pulling her own boot straps, the world would respect that and adjust to it. But to expect that the sole Super Power of today would invest in a large country like India to develop it as a counter weight to another large nuclear weapons country, and a neighbour to boot, is not only unrealistic, but reflects a failure to understand history. It is unbelievable that the Prime Minister would expect the US would appreciate India's need for nuclear weapons, and in fact hope to enhance India's capability to match China's in this area.

Vajpayee's letter hence confirmed, and placed in a disastrously negative perspective, the anti-China allegations frequently made by his free Tibet booter and Defence Minister, George Fernandes. Thus, the crystalizing effect of Vajpayee's letter, and the Chinese shift in tone from mild to harsh, in just four days after May 11, 1998 had shredded.

Sino-Indian normalization which had been in progress steadily since 1988. India's security posture against China should seek qualitative sufficiency and not be a search for parity. Despite Chinese missile deployments in Tibet and upgrading of surveillance capability in the Coco Islands (some 25 miles off the Andaman and Nicobar Islands), the strategist in India has to formulate a plan on the basis of present as well as emergent threats. The role of the political leadership has to harmonize that strategy with other dimensions of policy, and developments that would and could take place subsequently in the future.

China and India possess the second and the fourth largest military manpower in the world respectively. In terms of GDP evaluated at purchasing power parity rates, the ranking is the same: China ($4112.2 billion) and India ($2144.1 billion), ranking after US and Japan respectively. The London based

IISS estimates that in terms of manpower, the Chinese PLA is nearly double the size of the Indian army.

However, it may be noted that the Indian paramilitary forces, which have presently been deployed for border and internal security, could be, if required, deployed for other military purposes. China possesses an additional 1,00,000 manpower force for its strategic forces, which India does not have. However, the fact that India has 'gone nuclear', would mean that, in the near future, India needs to have a strategic force as well, if the avowed goal of "minimum deterrence" of the Indian government is to have content.

China has deployed about 60 per cent of its forces between the North and the East, which indicates Northeast Asia as being the immediate - concern of China, where the interests of three nuclear armed nations (US, Russia and China) intersect. The major deployment of the Indian forces is in the areas bordering China and Pakistan, with about 50 per cent deployment in the North and the East. India's paramilitary forces are also mostly deployed in these two areas.

China has deployed only about 100 per cent of its armed personnel in the areas bordering India, while India has more than half of its total armed forces in the Northern and Eastern periphery. The balance, in terms of personnel deployed, indicates a tilt in favour of India in case hostilities break out between the two. But of course, it is the strategy, tactics and morale that will ultimately decide the outcome in a war, and not arithmetic of armed forces.

In airforce capabilities of both countries, China, in terms of quantity, has a massive lead over the Indian airforce. However, qualitatively, China is not as far ahead of India. One major problem with India has been the lack of advanced trainer jets, causing a large number of crashes and premature deaths of young trained pilots.

China possess 74 submarines which include one nuclear powered Xia Class SSBN, carrying 12 BL-1 SLBMs. The bulk of the Chinese subsurface fleet is made up of the vintage Ming and Romeo classes which have limited offensive capabilities. Moreover, these vintage models are beset with problems such as lack of sonar capability, lack of adequate trained personnel, maintenance problems, etc.

Nearly two-thirds of the Indian underwater fleet is made up of the modern Soviet Kilo class submarines. The Indian fleet has undergone significant modernisation over the last decade. India has also inducted the German 1-209/1500 (HDW) with a view to replace the old Soviet made Foxtrot submarines. Submarines offer the best hope for India in a qualitatively equal nuclear force and second strike capability against China.

While China has the capability to lift some 8200 troops and 240 tanks through its .amphibious craft, India has the capability only to lift 2000 troops and 80 tanks. China has a massive lead in naval aviation units compared to India. However, Chinese naval aviation is completely land-based. This creates a disadvantage for China because it reduces the range of combat aircraft in maritime operations.

Indian naval capabilities have increased significantly both in numbers and quality. The proposed induction of a second aircraft carrier from Russia will enhance India's "blue navy" attack capability provided the repair work on the de-commissioned carrier is properly carried out. Presently, India has 2 squadrons with 20 Sea Harrier FRS-MKI each of maritime combat aircraft.

It may be noted here that despite huge lead over India in this category of naval weaponry, since China does not have 'blue water' fighting capability it does not pose a serious threat to India as yet from the Ocean. But the induction of nuclear armed submarines off the waters of Thailand would alter that position.

The planned acquisition by China, in the next few years, of multi-role combat aircraft, interceptors and submarines, and other airforce and navy weapon systems from countries like France, Britain and South Africa, will significantly enhance its capability vis-a-vis India, both in terms of numbers and quality. India, presently, does not have any major plans to match these.

India will need a phased modernisation plan of its airforce with a special focus on induction of more multi-role capable aircraft. India will also need to rethink its naval strategic doctrine and shift focus from surface forces to sub-surface forces. This arm of the navy is both cost-effective since India presently does not seem to face any major sea borne threat, except in exceptional circumstances from the US Seventh Fleet.

In hardware terms, the Chinese possess a massive lead over the Indians in all three arms of the military. Hence, in actual war fighting machine, China seems to have acquired a distinct edge over India. However, in case of a future armed conflict between the two, India's qualitatively more sophisticated navy and airforce, provides India a clear-cut option which if backed by a clear strategic military doctrine, can compensate for the imbalance in quantitative terms.

The pattern of deployment of forces however indicates that the immediate concern of China is the Asia-Pacific region, though there seems to be no conceivable immediate threat in that region. The focus that China is placing however may indicate its interest for other reasons. India, is currently faced with a two-front situation on the territories bordering Pakistan and China. That nexus considerably reduces the burden of security for China. How to disrupt that nexus, and reduce to a single front threat, requires a dexterity that the present leadership in India seriously lacks.

Estimation of China's defence spending is beset with many difficulties. It has been generally believed that, in the case of China, the actual defence expenditure is about 3.5 times the official figure. SIPRI analysis indicates that actual military expenditure has consistently been 1.7 to 1.8 times the official budget. However it also should be noted that in 1996, a Taiwanese analyst Wang Shao guang has debunked that view, and holds that based on 1993 data, the actual military expenditure was just 20 per cent higher than the official figure of 52.3 billion Yuan.

Despite these difficulties in exact assessment, a certain trend can be observed in its official defence allocation in China. There has been an annual average rise of 15.83 per cent during the six years between 1992 and 1998. However much of the increase in expenditure may have gone for creating better living conditions for the troops, something the PLA has been pressing for quite some time.

But the rise of the defence budget allocation in the last five years along with the plan to reduce manpower in the coming years, will however mean money for R&D and strengthening of strategic forces, in contrast to the Indian Defence allocations in which increases are largely accounted for by pay rise and pensions.

In the seven years since 1993 defence expenditure in India has grown from Rs. 175.81 billion to Rs. 457 billion (US $ 10.6

billion at prevailing exchange rates). It is believed that the main factors for the rise in expenditures were the implementation of the 4th and 5th Central Pay Commissions. This has absorbed most of the increases in defence spending leaving little for force modernisation and re-equipment during the past decade.

This also implies that, unless defence expenditure increases at a rate higher than during 1991-2000, available allocation for equipment, training and maintenance will be inadequate to meet the potential challenge of China, let alone the multiplier effect of a joint Sino-Pakistan axis. India cannot afford to be complacent about Chinese potential threat capacity for a long time to come. At the same time, neither 1962 should erode Indian confidence in dealing with the Chinese, and in facing the reality. The basic choice question however remains: Is China to be a future strategic collaborator with India, or does India perceive confrontation with China? Whatever choice India makes thus, should be free from short-term consideration and from fear of Chinese invincibility.

There is no basis for the Indian strategist to be weighed down by the general impression that the People's Liberation Army (PLA) is an invincible formidable force. This is a hangover from 1962 that is yet to be erased from Indian consciousness. Obviously China appears to have taught the "lesson" it had wanted, instead of India learning the lesson it should. The current impression about PLA is not based on a realistic assessment. Sreedhar, a Senior Research Associate in the Institute of Defence Studies and Analysis, New Delhi, has researched on this subject and we rely on his findings here.

The main question is whether a close scrutiny of the PLA's performance during the past 50 years validates the Indian hangover. During Chairman Mao's reign, the PIA had seen action five times—three times to fight a war with neighbours, once to fight the US "imperialism," and once to occupy the Paracel Islands in the South China Sea. The first action was in 1950-51, when the PLA met with the US forces head on in the Korean War. Whatever may be the counter claims, the PIA was perceived to have suffered heavy casualties and its advance south of the 38th parallel stopped. Some argue that the technological superiority of the US-led UN forces played the decisive role in this defeat of the PLA, but the casualty suffered by US troops were found unacceptable by a then War-Weary American public. This had diverted public attention from the real performance of the PLA.

A decade later, China decided to commit the use of force on the Sino-Indian border. In October 1962, the PLA moved in swiftly, defeated the Indian Army and declared unilateral ceasefire after taking possession of approximately 30,000 sq. km of Indian territory. Analysis, however, indicates that the Chinese succeeded largely in the Northeast border of India due to the failure of the Indian politico-military leadership to assess correctly the PLA's capabilities, and the collapse of the morale of senior Generals handpicked by Nehru and Menon. Had the Indian Air Force been pressed into action then, the course of the Sino-Indian war of 1962 could have been different. In fact, at the time, C. Rajagopalachari, free India's first Governor General, had advocated the deployment of the Air Force by India to destroy the supply lines of the Chinese Army, which were long into Tibet and threatened by the imminent severe winter on the Himalayan peaks and Tibetan plateau. Thus 1962 was more a defeat of Nehru and his myopia on China by the PLA on the ground.

In September 1967, the PLA confronted the Indian armed forces at Nathu La, on the Sikkim-Tibet border. The six-day "border skirmishes" from September 7 to 13, 1967, included exchange of heavy artillery fire when the PLA soldiers tried to cross that border in large numbers.

The attack was repulsed at all points. The PLA had received a severe mauling in the artillery duels across the barbed wire fence boundary. Indian gunners scored several direct hits on Chinese bunkers, including a command post from where the Chinese operations were being directed.

The Chinese army suffered at least twice as many casualties as the Indians in this encounter. From the Nathu La episode on the Sikkim-Tibet border, the Indian armed forces demonstrated beyond doubt that the PLA had been matched. This was clearly reflected in the unconditional ceasefire proposed by India fin a note delivered to the Chinese on September 12, 19671, all along the Sikkim-Tibet border from 05.30 hrs on September 13. Though officially, the Chinese rejected this unilateral ceasefire offer by India, there was subsequently a lull along the border.

On March 2-3, 1969, there were "border skirmishes" in the area of border post on the Ussuri River. The intruding PLA men were confronted by the Soviet Red Army and a stalemate ensued.

Again, on March 15, 1969, the PLA launched a fresh attack with an infantry regiment strength (estimated to be 2,000 men) with support units at Damansky Island on the Ussuri River. At first the Chinese succeeded in penetrating the island under cover of artillery and mortar fire from their side of the river, but a massive retaliation by the Red Army restored the status quo ex ante.

In a swift move, the PLA captured a disputed Paracel Islands in the South China Sea in 1974. With the ongoing conflict in Indo-China at that time, the Association of South-East Asian Nations (ASEAN) and Vietnam, who also claim part of these islands, did not offer any resistance to the PLA's occupation of the islands. Virtually without firing a shot, this time the PLA achieved total success.

'In the now famous February 1979 war with Vietnam, Chairman Deng announced that he wanted "to teach a lesson" to the Vietnamese. But in the ensuing Sino-Vietnam war, the PLA was badly mauled and forced to retreat. The battle hardened Vietnamese with better strategy and motivation were able to take on the PLA and inflict heavy casualties. Chairman Deng, a pragmatist, realised that there was need to improve the technological superiority of the PLA.

Consequently, the military modernisation segment of the Four Modernisation Programme (the other Curee being agriculture, industry, and science and technology) was initiated. Accordingly, greater allocations for defence in the Chinese budget, well disguised, have been made. The PLA decision-making apparatus has also been re-structured in the 1990s.

In mid-1986, it came to the notice of India that the PLA had built a helipad at Wandung in Sumdorong Chu Valley in Arunachal Pradesh. India reacted swiftly and the PLA had an eyeball-to-eyeball confrontation with the Indian Army in Sumdorong Chu Valley of Arunachal Pradesh in August 1986. After a week of tense moments both sides mutually agreed to withdraw their forces inside their respective territories and create a no-man's land. The Chinese posture at that time clearly indicated that Beijing quickly realised that 1962 could not be repeated. Afterwards, the PLA's official organ, Liberation Army Daily, wrote about the 'new' professionalism in the Indian armed forces. This paved the way for the 1988 Rajiv Gandhi visit, and the Chinese willingness to talk seriously.

The Nansha islands (the Spratlys) consist of about 150 reefs, sandbanks and islands in the South China Sea, 350 km from Vietnam's coast and 1,000 km from China. They straddle busy shipping lanes and are, therefore, strategically important. In addition, the preliminary geological surveys have shown that this area has vast deposits of crude oil and natural gas.

Both China and Vietnam claimed the Spratlys for centuries, but up to 1987 had been content with a war of words.

On March 14, 1988, the PLA's Navy clashed with the Vietnamese Navy for the first time. Though it was a very short confrontation, both sides suffered considerable numbers of casualties. In late March 1983, a war-weary Vietnam proposed bilateral talks with China to resolve the issue, but the Chinese rejected the offer.

However, fresh tensions erupted in May 1992, when the Chinese authorities leased on oil concession to an American firm, Creston Energy for oil exploration in and around the Spratlys, and Vietnam took strong objection to it. Soon enough, China chose to agree to bilateral talks with Vietnam.

From 1993 onwards, both China and Vietnam started negotiations. It is enough to say that the PLA was not able to enforce its authority to the extent it wanted to in the Spratlys, and to overrun the Vietnamese.

The PLA success story is also due to the timing of the campaign like in the Paracel Islands. An assessment of these PLA actions indicates that whenever the PLA confronted an adversary without any element of surprise, its performance was poor. This is clear from the Korean war, and the Nathu La and Ussuri incidents. In fact, in the Nathu La and Ussuri incidents, the PLA did not offer even stiff resistance. From all accounts it made a retreat the instant the adversary offered stiff resistance or acted "decisively."

Since 2012, the China-Vietnam tension has eased, and in its place, the Sino-Japenese face off has commenced. The South China Sea Islands claims of China and rejection of the Japanese of these claims need not however concern us as Indians. Japan has a super power cover, namely of US, and hence even though Japan in Asian, India has little materially to offer. From my point of view, it is a fact that after World War II ended, us, had handed over these Islands to the Chinese, but snatched it back after the Korean War.

This analysis ought not make India once again complacent, but could instill some confidence in dealing with China. The fundamental strategic position in the present situation, is that it is the compact or China with Pakistan which provides the necessary force multiplier makes China (or Pakistan) formidable. On the other hand, an induced Sino-Indian proper understanding would dramatically change the strategic and economic map of Asia. How India does that is the key question.

In this final analysis, it would be appropriate to quote Deng Xiaoping's statement made at his meeting with Prime Minister Rajiv Gandhi in Beijing on December 21, 1988:

"In recent years there has been comment about the next century being the Asia-Pacific century, as though its arrival is imminent. I do not agree with this viewpoint. When we talk of the Asia-Pacific region, if the United States is excluded then we find that only Japan, the 'four small dragons', Australia, and New Zealand are comparatively developed, and yet, they have 200 million people at most. Even if the far eastern region of the Soviet Union and the western part of the United States and

Canada are included, the population only comes to only about 300 million, whereas the combined population of our countries is 1.8 billion. If India and China fail to develop, it cannot be called an Asia century." The Selected Works of Deng Xicioping, Vol. III, excerpts from Beijing Review (Beijing), January 17-23, 1994.

India's most important diplomatic and strategic goal is thus, to disrupt this Sino-Pakistan compact. Recent developments offer some hope because despite the fact of China's significant contribution to Pakistan's nuclear and missile programmes, the Pakistani increased Inter Services Intelligence (ISI) support to the Uighur Muslims, in exploiting the ethnic and religious tension in the Xinjiang province and in providing conduct though Pakistan for Osama Bin Laden in served Al Qaeda terrorists has deeply concerned China. Pakistan might become a vortex of religious fervour of Central Asia. When that happens, China would then reassess its security relations with India, opening the possibility of strategic cooperation against terrorism and fundamentalism. India has to position herself for that now.

It is towards this end of plugging the 'security hole' in Xinjiang, recognizing that a flood of fundamentalism from the Central Asian Republics and Afghanistan could inundate the province, that China in a preemptive move has constituted the 'Shanghai Five', which interestingly does not include Pakistan.

The "Shanghai Five" forum and later SCO, originally comprised of Russia, China, Kazakhstan, Uzbekistan and Tajikistan. It was established at a meeting in Shanghai in April 1996. The dismantling of the Soviet Union had given birth to the Russian Federation and the five newly independent Central Asian republics, facing problems of disputed borders and overlapping ethnic communities. While, they had created the Commonwealth of Independent States (CIS) to deal with these problems. Three of these Central Asian republics—Kazakhstan, Kyrgystan and Tajikistan—had inherited disputed borders and overlapping ethnic communities with the Chin:

The Shanghai Five forum has been successful in putting in place a series of impressive confidence building measures (CBMs), and have now also resolved their border disputes with the Chinese. The Shanghai Five forum is relevant for India, because having resolved these immediate problems, the Forum has since then begun to expand the agenda to larger issues that impinge on the security and stability of the Asia-Pacific region.

In an interesting analysis, Dr. Swaran Singh of the IDSA, New Delhi has analysed how China will face the new but formidable problem of today: Islamic fundamentalism, which flourishes in Afghanistan and Tajikistan and has direct implications for China's sensitive Xinjiang province (831. But, ethnic violence has also since come to be recognised as a major problem by the Central Asian Republics, thus obtaining for China a joint platform to deal with this menace. Terrorism has since come to be the common issue of the greatest concern between China and these Republics. This is because these Republics have been formed on the basis of ethnic identity and have virtually recharged separatist sentiments among China's minorities living in its Western provinces like Gansu, Qinghai, and its autonomous regions of Ningxia, Tibet, and especially Xinjiang. China is known to have a whole host of ethnic groupings which have Central Asian origins and which have been nursing grievances against Beijing's nationality policies for a very long time.

China shares borders with Kazakhstan, that had inherited the second largest nuclear and missile stockpiles (next only to

Russia). But in 1995 Kazakhstan and Uzbekistan signed the Nuclear Non-Proliferation Treaty (NPT) as non-nuclear countries, which satisfied China. This is precisely what China now wants in South Asia: India to sign the NPT as a non-nuclear country. Pakistan would then follow suit.

More recently, because of their linkages with the Afghan politics, terrorism has come to be of China's critical concern.

Afghanistan is the main reason for instability in bordering states of Tajikistan, Uzbekistan and Turkmenistan, which thus has implications for China's security. Therefore, how China manages its relations with Central Asia has significance for its future relations with other Muslim states in the Middle East and South Asian region.

In the 1990s, Beijing had laid stress on the issue of transnational terrorism in bilateral meetings with Iran and Pakistan. But curiously, despite India's best efforts, China has declined to include terrorism as a subject in any joint communique with India. When President of India, K.R. Narayanan paid an official visit to Beijing (May 27-30, 2000), China flatly rejected drafts of joint statement prepared by India which included cross-border terrorism as a topic. Again in September 2000, when the UN Secretary General con-vened a meeting on Afghanistan, India despite being a neighbour was not invited. But Iran and Pakistan were. The Chinese hand is thus clearly visible.

The downtrend in US involvement with Central Asian Republics after these nations complied with the NPT, has since been providing China with an opportunity to step in, which China seized from the first tour of Central Asia by the then Premier, Li Peng, in April 1994. During his first official trip in 1998, Chinese President Jiang Zemin promised these countries access to Chinese port facilities. He offered to revive the Silk Route. Following these assurances, the Central Asian Republics have since begun trade with the Republic of Korea, Japan, the United States, Australia, Thailand and Malaysia through Chinese ports. They plan to export energy and minerals to third countries via northern Chinese ports. Turkmenistan also plans to lay a natural gas pipeline across China to Japan.

Without doubt, therefore the Shanghai Five Forum has been the most important creation that has facilitated China's interests and security concerns in south west region.

During the 1998 summit at Almaty (Kazakhstan), of the Forum, China succeeded in getting through a resolution where all agreed to reject religious extremism and to ban on their territories such activities harmful to the sovereignty, security and public order of any of the five countries. The 1999 summit was held at Bislikek (Kyrgystan), urged all nations to jointly fight international terrorism, ethnic separatism and religious fundamentalism. And the most recent fifth summit at Dushanbe (Tajikistan) on July 5, 2000, reiterated the agreement to jointly fight international terrorism, ethnic separatism and religious fundamentalism, and to set up a Regional Center in Tajikistan to study these problems.

Xinjiang remains the most important factor determining China's views about the Central Asian region. The fact that these Republics were broadly formed by disintegrating the USSR, the basis of their ethnic composition has encouraged China's minorities like Uighurs, Tibetans, Mongols, Kazakhs to accelerate their efforts for seeking self-determination, which caused increased unrest and violence in these regions during the early 1990s. In Xinjiang Uighur Autonomous Region, where Uighurs (Turkic Kazakhs) constitute the majority the turbulent Turkic-Muslim community shares common tradition and culture with the neighbouring Muslim Republics, impacting on China's ethnic unity, and its secular identity.

There had been earlier uprisings against Han China in 1933, 1944 and 1949 for the cause of establishing what was called "Republic of East Turkestan." It was the Qing dynasty which had annexed Xinjiang to China [571].

The majority of the 20 million Chinese Muslims live in Xinjiang where Uighurs alone numbered 7.2 million according to China's 1990 census. The second largest Muslim community are the Hui, who numbered 682,900. Uighurs have also been suspicious of Huis and see them as Han converts. But Huis who are found in every province of China have completely merged themselves in local communities and are not recognised as a separate community anywhere outside China. More specifically over 1.1 million nomadic Kazaks, who continue to have kin living in Central Asia's largest country Kazakhstan, also play a strong political role in Xinjiang Uighur Autonomous Region. The nomadic Kirghiz have kin in Central Asia's most democratic country, Kyrgyzstan. The small number of Uzbeks have kin living in the politically powerful country of Uzbekistan. Even, Xinjiang's Persian speaking Tajiks (33,500) are distantly related to Tajikistan.

Therefore, though Xinjiang's 530,000 sq. km area comprises one-sixth of mainland China, and have only a 15 million population, (i.e. 1.4 per cent of China's population) its ethnic and religious linkages to Central Asia makes Xinjiang Muslims critical in China's vision of the future.

China's policy to contain Islamic Fundamentalism can be thus broadly divided into two parts: (1) reviving the Silk Route as conduct for trade between China and Central Asia for ensuring China's continued access to Central Asian en-ergy resources and (2) creating the framework of 'Shanghai Five' forum which projects itself as an alternative paradigm for evolving the 21st century world order ensuring that ethnic linkages between the Republics and Xinjiang do not have any negative impact on China's internal security.

In view of Washington's now unfettered capacity to use issues like Tibet, Taiwan and human rights to weaken China, it has become imperative for China to ensure that any possibility of engineered social unrest does not affect its security and integrity (For a Chinese Perspective on this issue see [87]).

China's engagement with the Central Asian Republics thus is an attempt to provide Beijing with a buffer zone against the eastward expansion of NATO. Since the Kosovo War, China has felt squeezed from both West (NATO's Eastward expansion and its New Strategy) and West (US-Japan military alliance, the NMD, and its new interpretations).

The strategic question now for India is, given that the Chinese problem with Islamic Fundamentalism has the same root as India's if and how Indians can structure a common cause with the Chinese. The possibility that Islamic terrorism may bring China and India together has already begun to concern strategic thinkers in the West.

At Naval War College, Newport, Rhode Island a seminar was held on July 25 to August 4, 1999 to discuss a study on what Asia might look like in the year 2025. The scenarios in the study were stated by participants as speculative and imaginative descriptions of the future.

A scenario is the emergence of a "New Sino-Indian Condominium." In the lead-up to this development, the US tries but fails to reach a strategic arrangement with India till

2010. India resents US inattention, which feeds the Indian national psychology of wanting to be seen as a great power, the study visualised.

In a blatant act of self-assertion, India conducts a new round of nuclear tests in 2008, precluding any possibility of moving forward in a strategic relationship with the US. Growing anti-hegemonic sentiments stimulate India to accelerate its military buildup, shifting attention increasingly towards naval power.

As the US initiative towards India flounders and eventually collapses after India's nuclear tests, and as Indonesia's fragility becomes more threatening, India and China initiate strategic discussions on regional cooperation to secure sea-lanes, control regional unrest, and common concerns.... The anti-hegemonic undertones of their discussion gradually surface as an explicit shared objective in displacing the US from the regions they seek to dominate.

In 2014, Indonesia fragments, leading to a slaughter of wealthy Chinese, as separatist rebels seize Indonesian gas and oil production. "Everybody except China and India want the US to act to restore order" the study postulated.

In 2016, during the run-up to a US presidential election, a small band of Islamic militants, intent on hurting the US, fires, a series of powerful missiles at a US destroyer and frigate passing through the narrow Lombok Straits near Indonesia. More than 200 US sailors and marines are killed. All presidential candidates pledge to bring American troops home and the US announces immediate cessation of operations and order US ships to pull back.

In 2017, Chinese and Indian leaders intensify their discussion of ways to eject US presence from the South China

Sea, where China wants to establish its supremacy. They tacitly agree to cooperate and decide on joint action.

India moves rapidly into the Straits of Malacca, and China takes control of the Lombok and Sunda Straits and reopens them to international traffic. China also occupies the disputed Spratly Islands and Natuna gasfields. India's navy takes command of the Malacca Straits by cracking down on the pirates.

Most countries, including Japan, praise China and India for their joint action. Between 2017 and 2025, the US presence in the Pacific and Indian Oceans rolls back, and America's allies reach a new accommodation with China and India.

The tensions between China and India are not eliminated by their dividing much of Asia into hegemonic spheres. But for the time being, cooperation suits both perfectly.... The New Sino-Indian Order begins. The study suggests that Sino-Indian cooperation might be impeded if the US establishes a working strategic dialogue and common geopolitical objectives with one partner. "India appears to be the more logical choice of the two," the study says. It adds:

"US may need to rethink its strict non-proliferation policy, because some states like India which acquire nuclear weapons may actually contribute to the US national security goals ... the US may be faced with a trade-off between selective proliferation and regional presence."

A study of this kind is of course highly speculative, but that it was at all considered worthy of a seminar in a Naval War College in the US is indicative that the West has become concerned with the strategic fall-out from a possible Sino-Indian compact, however hypothetical it may seem at the moment. Now in retrospect, in 2018, it is India which has been cool to US advances especially in signing the path breaking

Four Foundational Agreement which Prime Minister Modi has agreed to sign, but has not so far. In the meantime the sudden summit in Wuhan in May 2018 has put the Four Foundational Agreements with US in Cold storage, although PM Modi has opened a new initiative with Indonesia in June 2018.

Given the strategic realignment of forces in Asia, India should reconfigure and recast its relationship with China. Rather than paint it as a clear and present danger, or a newfound ally, India needs to take the middle path in its interaction with China. This new policy should be grounded in pragmatism, not out of fear or overreaction. It should be derived from Indian and not Western assessments of China's strategic calculus, priorities and propensities, and India's position in that calculation. Once India's national interests are accordingly defined vis-a-vis China, the tasks for the foreign policy establishment becomes clear. It can contribute to both formulating the Indian response as well as implementing the resultant strategy. It must be stressed that just as India wishes to be liberated from ignominious comparisons with Pakistan, it needs to better calibrate its relations with China freeing it from odious and stexile comparison of arithmetic parity. Only then India will be able to play a larger role in Asian affairs, in a compact with China.

But for such a compact to become within the realm of possibilities requires a change in the mindset of the Chinese and Indian leadership, and washing off the 1962 hangover. In particular, the new mindset would make the future Indian leaders to recognize that Pakistan despite its nuclear capability is not in India's league, and for China to recognize that India is very much in China's league and that it is no more possible for China to 'teach any lesson' to India, without, itself coming to grief.

# CHAPTER 4

# Conclusions

## 1. CONCLUDING COMMENTS

"Nothing in my long political career," wrote Prime Minister Nehru to Premier Chou Enlai on October 27, 1962, "has hurt and grieved me more than the fact that the hopes and aspirations for peaceful and friendly neighbourly relations which we entertained and to promote which my colleagues in the Government of India and myself worked so hard ever since the establishment of the People's Republic of China, should have been shattered by the hostile and unfriendly twist given on India-China relations during the past two years." Nehru was 'hurt and grieved', because he had gone out of his way not only to befriend China, but to plead the cause of China in the councils of the world, advocated her admission to U.N., and all along opposed the military pacts which were set up to isolate China. Clearly Nehru India's China perspective was based on *ad hocism* and noblesse oblige psychology, and not on *real politik.* No wonder, his illusions came crashing on him at the fag end of his long career as Prime Minister of India.

The Border Dispute was an entirely new Chapter in the long history of otherwise peaceful and friendly relations between China and India. Far from any political conflicts or territorial claims history records that for centuries the remarkable absence of disputes between the two biggest and neighbouring countries of Asia which are also the two most populated countries of the world. For eight to ten years after 1949, the relations between the two countries also seemed extremely cordial. But only apparently so, since the seeds of discord had been sown early in 1954. How these seeds germinated since then is described in Chapter 3. The core inference from the facts therein is simply this: Neither India, nor indeed China have a case of any merit on the Border Dispute and neither had been honest to the other about it throughout the decade of the 1950s.

It was on January 23, 1959 that Mr. Chou Enlai (in a letter to Nehru) had for the first time questioned in writing the cartographic boundary between India and China. Even then, he made no specific territorial claims. The claim to 50,000 square miles of territory was put forward by Chou Enlai only on September 8, 1959. The question was not raised earlier even though the Government of India had made public declarations affirming the "established boundaries" of India, and published maps in 1954 accordingly.

The Government of China had not revealed their territorial claims, even when the two countries negotiated and signed the 1954 Agreement on Tibet. Though it was an agreement on trade and intercourse, it was concluded to settle all outstanding issues and to consolidate the friendly relations between the two countries. The Preamble to this Agreement indicates the wider purposes of the treaty. The Five Principles of Peaceful Co-existence were embodied in it for the first time. One of the Five Principles was "mutual respect for each other's territorial integrity and sovereignty," which clearly implied that the borders of each party to the treaty were known to the other. Had China believed that there was a territorial dispute of any size about the entire Sino-Indian boundary, that was the time to raise the question when the two countries were solemnly pledging to respect mutually the "territorial integrity" of the other.

In October 1954, when the Prime Minister Nehru visited China, he had mentioned to the Chinese leaders that he had seen some maps published in China which showed a wrong boundary between the two countries, and added that he was not worried about it, because the boundaries of India were quite clear and not a matter of argument! file Chinese Prime Minister had replied that these maps were "reproductions of old maps drawn before 1949" and they had no time to revise them. Again, in 1956, when Chou Enlai visited India, Nehru referred to the wrong Chinese maps, especially in relation to the Eastern Sector. Chou Enlai then had said that he had accepted the McMahon Line as the border between China and Burma, and he would accept this border with India also. Or so Nehru believed he said so. As late as 1958, the Government of India drew the attention of the Chinese authorities to a map published in an official Chinese magazine, which included in Chinese territory four of the five Divisions of India's North-East Frontier Agency, some areas in Uttar Pradesh in the Middle Sector and large areas in Ladakh. It was pointed out that as the Chinese Communist Government had been in power for nearly nine years, 'corrections' in Chinese maps were overdue. Thus, even when India had raised the matter of these wrong maps, the Chinese did not even suggest that the boundary, was in any manner under dispute.

On January 23, 1959, Chou Enlai wrote to Nehru admitting that it was "true that the border question was not raised in 1954 when negotiations were being held between Chinese and Indian sides for the Agreement on Trade and

Intercourse between Tibet region of China and India. This was because conditions were not yet ripe for its settlement." This is an amazing admission. And why did time become 'ripe' in 1959 for the dispute to be raised? That Premier Chou did not make clear in the letter.

In 1957, the Chinese built a road across the Aksai Chin area. An Indian patrol in the area was detained by the Chinese in the summer of 1958 and in reply to a protest, the Chinese referred to their "frontier guards" having detained the Indian patrol because they were in "Chinese territory." The following year, a Chinese PLA force came to Khurnak Fort in Ladakh, arrested an Indian patrol party in Aksai Chin.

In October 1959, they further penetrated into Ladakh and opened fire on an Indian patrol near the Rongka Pass, killing nine. Ten others were taken into custody. China had thus, by 1959, already begun to resort to force qualified by any adjective: defensive or offensive. The question is why?

On February 8, 1960, the Prime Minister of India wrote to Premier Chou Enlai suggesting a meeting between the two. The meeting took place in April 1960, but it confirmed the serious differences in regard to the understanding of even basic facts about the border after a decade of interaction between the two countries. The Prime Ministers, therefore, agreed that the officials of the two Governments should meet and examine relevant documents and make a joint report, and that, in the meantime, every effort he made to "avoid friction and clashes on the border." The Government of India published that Report in February 1961, and Government of China published it in April 1962. The Officials' Report is a unique document of its kind, and serves even today as the basic source material on the border dispute between China and India.

But in July 1962, in a new turning point, Chinese troops encircled an Indian post in the Galwan Valley. There were also other clashes. Nevertheless, on July 26, 1962, the Government of India informed the Chinese Government that India was prepared to enter into discussions on the basis of the Officials' Report. While notes on preliminary discussions to ease the tension were being exchanged, the Chinese troops, on September 8, 1962, marched across in the Eastern Sector, viz., the McMahon Line. This was followed on October 20, 1962 by massive onslaught by China in both the Western and Eastern Sectors of the border, overwhelming the Indian forward posts, as the Chinese armies marched, even by Chinese maps, well inside Indian territory.

On October 24, 1962, Premier Chou Enlai put forward his three-point proposals for cease-fire and disengagement. India made a counter-proposal, that the status quo on the border, as of September 8, 1962, be restored, and thereafter the two countries should enter into discussions. The Chi-nese rejected that but then, dramatically, on November 21, China announced their unilateral cease-fire and withdrawal from Indian territory. Accordingly, the Chinese forces with-drew 20 km behind the McMahon Line, which they called "the 1959 line of actual control" in the Eastern Sector, and also 20 km behind the line of their latest position in Ladakh, which they further identified with the so-called "1959 line of actual control" in the Western Sector. This left the Chinese in possession of 14,500 square miles of territory in Ladakh. India declined to accept these unilateral terms but stated that she would not disturb the ceasefire. At the same time, India asked for restoration to the status quo ante of September 8, 1962 in all sectors of the boundary, as a condition precedent for a mutually-agreed ceasefire. A stalemate resulted, that in effect remains so today.

In his last speech to the session of the All India Congress Committee in Bombay on May 17, 1964, ten days before his demise, the Prime Minister Nehru said that India was prepared to negotiate with China if the Chinese Government agreed to remove their posts in Ladakh. He added that the initiative lay with China and that it was now for her "to take steps and say something."

On May 19, Xinhua, the New China News Agency, dismissed Nehru's call as another 'precondition' and as an 'obstacle' raised by India to the holding of negotiations. Xinhua, the official agency, went further and claimed that the 20 km demilitarised area had always been Chinese territory, and that there was no question of China withdrawing her posts in "her own territory."

Towards the end of December 1964, Prime Minister Chou Enlai, speaking to the National People's Congress in Beijing, decisively and finally rejected the idea of holding talks between the two countries on the basis of "no posts of either side" in the demilitarised zone in Ladakh. He called the suggestion "an unreasonable Indian precondition" and declared that China would never dismantle its posts from this area. The Chinese Prime Minister, in the speech, also reminded India that China had not relinquished its claim to 90,000 sq. kilometres of India territory south of the McMahon Line. This territorial demand was in addition to the 23,200 sq. km. of territory in Ladakh already with China by then.

## INDIA'S CHINA PERSPECTIVE

The perspective on China in India today is at one end one of an aggressive and expansionist threat. At the other extreme, is that of China as a sister ancient civilization. Most Indians however carry in their minds both caricatures. This causes wild swings in moods in Indian public perception influenced by reports in the media of Chinese 'unfriendliness' or alternatively of superficial 'warm gestures' such as the 1970 Chairman Mao's smile at an official reception. This causes the cyclic movements in policy towards China that we have seen over the last five decades, and has sown confusion in China as well as destabilized our relations with that country.

The first requirement therefore of an effective Indian policy towards China is to build a national consensus on how we define our complex of interests vis-a-vis China, in a world that has dramatically changed since 1962.

China's negative perceptions of India is articulated by the 1962 armed conflict: That it was the result of Indian unreasonableness; that India wanted to inherit the ill gotten concessions obtained by British Imperialist from a weak China; India is not reconciled to the situation in Tibet notwithstanding recognizing Tibet as an autonomous region of China; that India is seeking domination of South Asia; and that India is deliberately using the "myth" of a Chinese threat to find a pretext for its nuclear pursuit in defiance of the formed international opinion, and to become a global power thus with the patronage of the US, which increasingly is turning to developing options to contain China.

## CONCLUSION

As the new millennium begins, there exists substantial economic gap between China and India. But if India were to concentrate on producing a significantly accelerated growth in agriculture, information technology, services, and exports during the next two decades, the gap can be quickly bridged because of the clear plateauing of Chinese growth rate in the 1990s. Clearly, India will have to make strenuous efforts fiscally, to raise the rate of investment to reach or cross 30 per cent, as a minimum condition to commence on closing the China-India gap. The task of course is within reach and it is a target for which the Indian people would be willing to make a sacrifice. "Catching up with China" is a worth-while slogan for India's new millennium, along with a national commitment to grow at 10 percent per year. Both goals are feasible and attainable, within India's grasp, and at striking distance. The only question is whether the policy is upto it, or will it sink further into the communal and fundamentalist morass that it is already knee deep in.

Whether or not India becomes a global power in the 21st century depends on India alone that would require in the country a combination of political unity, economic growth, social cohesion, credible military capability and shrewd diplomacy. It is not a status anybody can then deny India. But by the same token, no power is going to confer that status on India until then. Thus, if in the years ahead, India fails to attain global status, it will be clue to its domestic and diplomatic failures, and not due to any international perfidy or lack of patronage. Such a global status would have a multiplier effect if India is also able to harmonize its interests with China and live in peace with this neighbour. The question is how such an harmonization can come about.

Tibet will continue to play the determining role in Sino-Indian. relations. In the Joint Press Communiqué issued on

December 23, 1988, at the end of Prime Minister Rajiv Gandhi's visit to China, the Indian government had reiterated its policy regarding Tibet, an autonomous region of China, and that anti-China political activities by Tibetan elements would not be permitted on Indian soil. The statements were repeated during the subsequent exchange of visits by the Prime Ministers of China and India, in 1993 and 1996. While beyond this it is not possible for India to accommodate China's wishes, if any, e.g., relating to the presence of the Dalai Lama in India, nevertheless the statements of the Indian Prime Minister has to have transparent content before India can expect reciprocal action from China to settle other pending issues.

India does not however have easy options on Tibet. It can err in two opposite directions. On the one hand, under Chinese pressure the Government may be tempted to make Tibetans feel unwelcome, and even force them to leave. On the other, in misguided megalomania, support the freedom for Tibet as demanded by Dalai Lama's Bureau. Both these options are not in India's interest. India thus has to define its perspective on China with clarity and transparency: Does India want a compact with China in the twenty-first century (Choice I), or does India want to participate in the growing prospect to contain China (Choice II)?

This volume has compiled enough historical material to show that till 1959, India's relation with China was for centuries remarkably free from conflict and one of friendly cultural borrowing, something unprecedented in world history. One has to study the history of Europe or West Asia to see the contrast. The Indian and Chinese people at one level have internalized their mutual respect for each other's civilization.

This internalized sentiment has to surface and be the cementing force in future relations, free from the deception of the recent past. Besides, the China containment policies of the 1950s and 1960s has not served India's security interests. At a crucial moment, e.g., in earlier 1971 during the Bangladesh Liberation war; when China made threatening gestures in support of Pakistan, India was abandoned by the Super Powers who had earlier jointly advocated containment of China. The US, for example, had despatched a task force of the US Naval Seventh Fleet into the Bay of Bengal to deter India in proceeding further in Bangladesh (then part of Pakistan). The US, incidentally, has despite all the anti-China rhetoric of 1950s, never has supported an Independent Tibet, despite vociferous material and verbal support for the Dalai Lama.

My conclusion thus is that from cultural, historical and strategic perspectives, the maximum and stable strategic gains to India in the 21st century obtains in Choice I. How that should be structured is a matter of detail and will be analysed in a subsequent volume. In this volume, my concern has been to portray the China reality from Indian perspective is as close to the truth as possible. But clearly a trade-off between China's relations with Pakistan, and India's transparency in Tibet are the cornerstones of that structuring of policy. What Indian security needs Loclay is moderated, normal but not intimate, Sino-Pakistan relations, for which India has to offer as a trade-off a transparent commitment to respect China's interest in its own autonomous province of Tibet. This Indian commitment has value for China's strategic calculations especially in the context of China's recent growing vulnerability to Islamic Fundamentalism in Xinjiang province. It is however not as simple as that, since China values Pakistan as a reliable conduit to the warm waters of the Arabian Sea and the Indian Ocean.

Hence, India's China Strategio Perspective ought have a clear plan to build a defence capacity to potentially defeat a China-Pakistan possible joint aggression against India, while pursuing a vigorous diplomacy to persuade China to desist from any such eventuality while emphasizing the terror green houses of Pakistan. In other keep our eyes open while wooing China into a strategic partnership with India.

## PERSPECTIVES AND REVIEW

In short, after the establishment of the Peoples Republic on October 1, 1949, Chairman Mao led government recognised border settlement as a problem and declared eschewing attempts to regain "lost lands". China he said, would accept the border alignments with which history had left it, and negotiate where necessary to formalise and confirm them, in the spirit of "mutual understanding and mutual accommodation."

In India, it meant that India would retain the territory, up the McMahon Line, which the British Imperialists had negotiated with pre-Communist China in 1912. Instead of clinching the issue then as Sardar Patel in a long reasoned letter to Nehru had advised the latter instead went on a binge of international conference and patronising the China.

Nehru even surrendered India's leverage in Tibet by signing a treaty in 1954 accepting unconditionally China's sovereignty over Tibet, and surrendering India's Posts all over Tibet. From then on, Nehru's international patronising began to irritate China.

The 1956 Bandung Conference of Asian Nations sowed the seeds of distrust between the two nations, leading to the first inkling of trouble in 1958 when Beijing found itself accused of "aggression" when Indian border guards found a Tibetan/Chinese presence in small tracts claimed by India in what became known as the "middle sector" of the border on the boundary of Uttar Pradesh, India's largest province. This portion of the border was not demarcated by the McMahon Line.

In August 1959 a serious armed clash took place at Longju on the McMahon Line, in which an Indian border guards was killed. It set off an outburst of public anger and official statements critical of China.

The more serious clash in October 1959 at the Kongka Pass on the Kashmir/Xiankiang border, with killed on both sides, had a huge effect on Indian public opinion and jolted the Chinese leadership. By 1960 when Chinese Premier Zhou Enlai came to India to negotiate found a hostile Congress party leadership. He went back with empty hands.

By mid-1961, however, the newly formulated "Forward Policy" of using force to push back the Chinese troops from the tracts of territory claimed by India conducted by the Army rather than border armed police, were challenging Chinese posts and probing for positions from which to dominate and sever their lines of communication.

Towards the end of 1961 meeting of the Central Military Commission (CMC) was convened to consider the response to India's forward probing.

In March 1962 the CMC met again to reconsider the border situation. Indian troops were continuing to press forward in the Western sector, attempting to cut off Chinese posts and sometimes opening harrassing fire upon them. On the diplomatic front India was meeting every Chinese appeal for a mutual military standstill and negotiation with demands for unilateral Chinese withdrawal from all territory claimed by India. It was decided there should be no retreat under Indian pressure. When Indian troops established positions threatening Chinese posts in the western sector, additional Chinese forces should simply use their great advantage in manoeuvrability and numbers to outflank and dominate them in turn. Thus the two sides would be confronting each other in interlocking, mutually threatening positions. Chinese forces would still be forbidden to fire without permission from the central political authority. Since India was rejecting China's calls peaceful coexistence, Mao quipped, it should be confronted with "armed coexistence".

The summer of 1962 saw only intensification of that situation. Beijing sharpened its tone and heat of its diplomatic warnings and made its threats of counterforce more direct. Yet Premier Zhou Enlai asked Chen Yi, now foreign minister, to meet privately with the Indian defence minister, Krishna Menon, when they were in Geneva at an international conference, and sound him out about India's real intentions [see John Garver "China's Decision for War with India in 1962" in Alastair Iain Johnston and Robert S. Ross, editors, *New Directions in the Study of China's Foreign Policy,* Stanford University Press, 2006, pp. 86-130].

Chen reported that Menon had simply re-stated his government's position: e.g., Beijing's complaints were groundless since Indian troop were doing nothing more than advancing into their own territory; the international borders were clearly marked on India's maps and were fixed an final; therefore there was nothing to negotiate. Menon's tone was "arrogant", Chen added. According to sources, Zhou concluded, "It seem as though Nehru wants a war with us" [Minutes of the meeting in: *Cold War International History Project,* Vol. 13 (Fall/Winter 2001), pp. 264].

Meanwhile the forward policy had begun to be implemented in miniature in the north-east, with Indian forces advancing across the McMahon Line in such places as the Indians thought it necessary to correct McMahon's cartographic deficiencies. India's reoccupation of Longju in May prompted Beijing to warn that it would not "stand idly by" under such provocation – only to see another Indian post established across the McMahon Line near the trijunction with Bhutan. The Indian named it Dhola post.

On 8 September the Chinese extended their tactic of containment through "armed coexistence" to the recently established Dhola post north of the McMahon Line at its western extremity.

Reading that move as a deliberate incursion into Indian Territory (even though Indian government was aware that the threatened Indian post was well to the north of the map-marked McMahon Line), Nehru gave orders that the Chinese must be "thrown out". The Indian army was given orders to attack the Chinese troops threatening Dhola post and drive them off all the territory. Nehru publicly proclaimed his order as soon as he had it issued.

On 3 October Beijing sent its final diplomatic warning and plea for immediate, unconditional negotiation: India instantly rejected it.

On 18 October an expanded Politburo meeting of the Chinese Communist Party approved the PLA's operational plans and set 20 October as the day for action. In terms of international law Beijing could argue that in the circumstances, with Nehru having declared his belligerent intentions, and the Indian army, on 10 October, made its first offensive move in the Dhola area, China acted in "anticipatory self-defence".

Incompetent commanders appointed by the Nehru government on the Indian side, obeying politically motivated and tactically foolish directives from Delhi, quickly brought their own troops to defeat and rout.

Having achieved total victory in its campaign Beijing declared its pre-planned ceasefire on 21 November and all Chinese forces withdrew a few weeks later beyond the and north of the McMahon line.

Thus Nehru in 10 weeks self-destructed his "world leader" status assiduously built over a decade. India's China relations lay in tatters, while China rose to world power recognition in India's place. Now 56 years later, in 2018, India is yet to recover the lost ground of 1962, all due to the folly and vanity of one pretender.

In a nutshell thus, China would be more flexible in dealing with India if it became convinced of India's equidistance with the USA in Sino-US disputes distant places such as Taiwan and South China Sea Islands. Of course China must respond with similar non chalance on Pakistan-India disputes.

India has thus to develop deeper cultural and civilizational linkages with China and the rest of Asia as an important part of its diplomacy. India has to realise that it can't just be a spectator, or a mere visible participant, or even a 'pole' in the so-called multi-polar world. China has conceptualised and implemented the centrality of China by befriending all of India's neighbours and brought them on board in their OBOR proposal. We Indians should stop going delirious about the Anglo-American constructs such as bonding with US junior partners in their strategic games and the like, but instead focus on Asia and consolidate our influence therein.

The then President of China, Hu Jintao, had got adopted in the plenary session of the Communist Party of China in 2007 the goal of developing a "Harmonious Society" of blending spiritual values of Confuciousism and Taoism with aspiration for material progress.

This is similar to the Hindu values of placing on a pedestal the intellect and sacrifice [gyana and tyaga]. Since then China has proceeded systematically to bring countries of Asia under its influence with imaginative proposals such as OBOR and CPEC. India has been reduced to merely reacting to such proposals without any of her own to canvass as an alternative.

India therefore has to strive imaginatively become a stakeholder in this new paradigm. India has therefore to give up its reticence and passive diplomacy and learn to exercise power. Under PM Modi we have atleast conveyed to the world that we have arrived and are interested in carving out India's due place.

To some extent China has made that clear already by writing into CPEC and OBOR documents that the India objected road through PoK would be subject to the final solution of the Jammu and Kashmir so-called issue.

In my talks with Chinese personalities in Beijing, I had pointed out that J&K Maharaja had signed the Instrument of Accession and hence according to the Indian Independence Act of the House of Commons, the merger onto India is final and irrevocable. Nehru seeking UN intervention was without a Cabinet Resolution and hence is invalid.

In brief then India is now poised to form a global triangle with US and China, and therefore the Government must seize that opportunity which requires a serious effort at reconcilation with China in a give and take mode without sacrificing any of our national interest.

# References

**Books**


1. Bowie, Robert R. and Fairbank, John F *communist China, 1955-1959: Policy Documents With Analysis,* Cambridge, Massachusetts: Harvard University Press, 1965.
2. Brecher, Michael, *India and World Politics: Krishna Menon's View of the World,* New York: Frederick **A.** Praeger, 1968.
3. Bitzinger, R.A. and Ling Chong Pin, *The Defence Budget of the Peoples Republic of China* (Washington D.C. 1998).
4. Cantril, Albert H., *The Indian Perception of the Sino-Indian Border Clash,* Princeton: Institute for International Social Research, 1963.
5. Dalai Lama, *Freedom in Exile: An Autobiography,* Abacus, 1998, London.
6. Dalvi, J.D., *Himalayan Blunder. The Curtain-Raiser to the SinoIndian War of 1962,* Bombay: Thacker and Company, 1969.
7. Dass, Durga, *India: From Curzon to Nehru and After,* London: Collins Clear-Type Press, 1969.
8. (Ed.): *Sardar Patel's Correspondence* 1945-50, Vol. 8 (Ahmedabad, 1973), p. 8.
9. Doolin, Dennis J., *Territorial Claims in the Sino-Soviet Conflict,* Stanford: Stanford University Press, 1965.
10. Fisher, M.W., *et. al, Himalayan Battlefield: Sino-Indian Rival?), in Ladakh,* New York: Frederick A. Praeger, 1963.
11. Galbrath, John Kenneth, *Ambassador's Journal,* Boston: Houghton and Mifflin Company, 1969.
12. Ginsburg, George and Mathos, Michael, *Communist China and Tibet: The First Dozen Years,* The Hague: Martinus Nighoff, 1964.
13. Griffith, William, *The Sino-Soviet Territorial Claims in the Sino-Soviet Conflict,* Stanford: Stanford University Press, 1965.
14. Hutheesing, Raja, ed., *Tibet Fights for Freedom,* Bombay: Orient Longmans, 1960.
15. Jain, Girilal, *Panch Shila and After: A Reappraisal of Sino-Indian Relations*

*in the Context of the Tibetan Insurrection,* New York: Asia Publishing House, 1960.

16. Kaul, B.M., *The Untold Story,* Bombay: Allied Publishers, 1967.
17. Kavic, Lorne J., *India's Quest for Security: Defense Policies, 1947-1965,* Berkeley: University of California Press, 1967.
18. Kennedy, Robet F., *Thirteen Days: A Memoir of the Cuban Missile Crisis,* New York: Signet Books, 1969.
19. Khatri, Sunil: *Events Leading to the Sino-Indian Conflict of 1962,* IDSA Monograph Series No. 58, 2017.
20. Lamb, Alastair, *The McMahon Line,* London: Routledge and Kegan Paul, 1966.
21. *The China-India Border,* London: Faber and Faber, 1964.
22. *The Sino-Indian Border in Ladakh,* Columbia: University of South Carolina Press, 1975.
23. Macfarquhar, Roderick: (a) *The Politics of China,* Second Edition, Cambridge University Press, 1997: (1) Origins of tile cultural Revolution, 3, Oxford University Press, 1997.
24. Mankekar, D.R., *The Guilty Men of 1962,* Bombay: The Tulsi Shah Enterprises, 1968, Penguin Edition, 1998.
25. Maxwell, Neville, *India's China War,* New York: Pantheon Books, 1970.
26. Panikkar, K.M., *India and China:* A Study of Cultural Relations, Bombay: Asia Publishing House, 1957.
27. *Two Chinas: Memoirs of a Diplomat,* London: George Allen and Urwin, 1955.
28. Ranganathan C.V. and Vinod Khanna, *India and China: The Way Ahead,* Har-Anand Publications, New Delhi, 2000.
29. Richardson, High E., *Tibet and Its History,* London: Oxford University Press, 1962.
30. Strong, Louise Anna, *When Serfs Stood up in Tibet,* Peking: New World Press, 1965.
31. Thomas, Lowell Jr., *The Silent War in Tibet,* New York: Doubleday and Company, 1959.
32. Van Eckelen, W.F., *India's Foreign Policy and Border Dispute,* The Hague: Martinus Nighoff, 1964.
33. Wang Jia Nei and Nyima Gyain Cain: *The Historical Status of China's Tibet,* China Intercontinental Press, Beijing, 1997.
34. Woodman, Dorothy, *Himalayan Frontiers,* New York: Praeger Publishers, 1969.

35. Zagoria, Donald, *The Sino-Soviet Conflict, 1956-61,* Princeton: Princeton University Press, 1967.

**Articles**

36. Acharya, Alka, "Prelude to the Sino-Indian War: Aspects of Decision-Making Processes during 1959-62," *China Report,* Vol. 32, No. 4, October-December 1996, pp. 363-93.
37. Ahmad, Rafiq Karm, "India, China and Iran: Renewing Interaction Along the Old Silk Road," *Journal of International Affairs,* Vol. 2, Nos. 34, July-December 1995, pp. 66-83.
38. Ahmed, Abu Tahir Salahuddin, "India-China Relations in the 1990s," *Journal of Contemporary Asia,* Vol. 26, No. 1, 1996, pp. 100-115.
39. Bakshi, Z.C., "Sino-Indian Relations in the 1990s," *USI Journal,* Vol. 122, No. 510, October-December 1992, pp. 450-55.
40. Bissenden, Rosemary, "India and the Northern Frontier," *Australian Outlook,* 14 April, 1960, pp. 15-19.
41. Brecher, Michael, "Nehru's Foreign Policy and the China-India Conflict Revisited," *Pacific Affairs,* Vol. 50, No. 1, Spring 1977, pp. 99-106.
42. Bristow, Damon, "Mutual Mistrust Still Hampering Sino-Indian Rapprochement, *Jane's Intelligence Review,* Vol. 9, No. 8, August 1997, pp. 368-71.
43. Came, Sir Olaf, "Sino-Indian Border," *Asian Review,* London, January 1960.
44. "The Geography and Ethics of India's Northern Frontiers," *777e Geographical Journal,* CXXVI, Part 3 (September, 1960), pp. 298-309.
45. Chakrabarti, Sreemathi, "China and Naxalites: An Inquiry into Direct Contacts and Dissemination of Chinese Propaganda in India," *China Report,* Vol. 22, No. 3, July-September 1986, pp. 211-32.
46. Chengappa, B.M., "India-China Relations: Issues and Implications," *Strategic Analysis,* Vol. 16, No. 1, April 1993, pp. 39-52.
47. *China Pictorial Magazine,* No. 95 (July, 1958), pp. 20-21.
48. Cohen, Stephen P., "India's China War and After," *Journal of Asian Studies,* Vol. 30, 1971, pp. 847-57.
49. Duncan, George T., and Randolph M. Siverson, "Markov Chain Models for Conflict Analysis: Results from Sino-Indian Relations, 1959-64," *International Studies Quarterly,* Vol. 19, No. 3, September 1975, pp. 343-74.

50. Dutta, Sujit, "China's Emerging Power and Military Role: Implications for South Asia" in Jonathan D. Pollack and Richard H. Yang, eds., *In China's Shadow: Regional Perspectives on Chinese Foreign Policy and Military Development,* Santa Monica: RAND Corporation, 1998, pp. 91-114.
51. Fairbank, J.K. and Tang, S.K., "On the Ching Tributary System," *Harvard Journal of Asiatic Studies,* 6 June, 1941, pp. 135-246.
52. Fischer, Margaret W., and Leo E. Rose, "Ladakh and the Sino-Indian Border Crisis," *Asian Survey,* Vol. 2, February 1962, pp. 27-37.
53. Foot, Rosemary, "Chinese-Indian Relations and the Process of Building Confidence: Implications for the Asia-Pacific," *Pacific Review,* Vol. 9, No. 1, 1996, pp. 58-76.
54. "Sources of Conflict Between China and India As Seen From Beijing" in Sumit Ganguly and Ted Greenwood, eds., *Mending Fences: Confidence-and Security-Building Measures in South Asia,* Boulder: Westview Press, 1996, pp. 57-72.
55. Ganguly, Sumit, "The Sino-Indian Border Talks, 1981-89: A View From Delhi," *Asian Survey,* Vol. 29, No. 12, December 1989, pp. 1123-35.
56. Garver, John W., "The Indian Factor in Recent Sino-Soviet Relations," *China Quarterly,* No. 125, March 1991.
57. "Sino-Indian Rapprochment and the Sino-Pakistan Entente," *Political Science Quarterly,* Vol. 111, No. 2, 1996, pp. 322-47.
58. Gladney D.N., "Muslim Face of China," *Current History,* Vol. 92, No. 575, September 1993, Philadelphia, USA.
59. Green L.C., "Legal Aspects of the Sino-Indian Frontier," *The China Quarterly,* No. 3 (July-September, 1960), pp. 42-58.
60. Harrigan, Anthony, "Seapower in History: India and China," *Contemporaly Review,* Vol. *228,* No. 1332, M: Irch, pp. 132-38.
61. Horn, Robert C., "Soviet Union and Sino-Indian Relations," *Orbis,* Vol. 26, No. 4, Winter 1983, pp. 47-59.
62. Hu, Qingyun, "Zhong Yin Bianjie Zhanzheng" (The Sino-Indian Border War), in Zhongguo Geming Lishi Bowuguan Dangshe Yanjiushi, *Dangshi Yanjiu Ziliao* (Materials on Party History), No. 11, 1990.
63. Hu Shill, "The Indianisation of China: A Case Study in Cultural Borrowing, Independence, Convergence and Borrowing," *Harvard University Tercentenary Publications,* Cambridge, Mass, 1937, p. 247.
64. Karnad, Bharat, "Getting Tough with China: Negotiating Equitable not 'Equal' Security," *Strategic Analysis,* Vol. 21, No. 10, January 1998, pp. 1429-41.

65. Katrak, Savak, "India's Communist Party Split," *The China Quarterly,* No. 7 (July-September, 1961), pp. 138-47.
66. Levi, Werner, "China and the Two Great Powers," *Current History,* Vol. 39, (December, 1960), pp. 321-26.
67. "Chinese-Indian Competition in Asia," *Current History,* Vol. 39, No. 222, February 1960, pp. 65-68, 81.
68. "China-India Relations in the post-Soviet Era: The Continuing Rivalry," *China Quarterly,* No. 142, June 1995, pp. 317-55.
69. Liao, Kuang-Sheng and Whiting, Allen, "Chinese Press Perceptions of Threat: The U.S. and India, 1962," *The China Quarterly,* Vol. 53 (January-March, 1973), pp. 80-87.
70. Mansingh, Surjit, "India-China Relations in the post-Cold War era," *Asian Survey,* Vol. 34, No. 3, March 1994, pp. 285-300.
71. Maxwell, Neville, "India's Forward Policy," *The China Quarterly,* No. 45 (January-March, 1971), pp. 157-58.
72. "The Sino-Indian Border Dispute Reconsidered," *Economic and Political Weekly,* April 10, 1999 p. 905.
73. "China and India: The Unnegotiated Dispute," *The China Quarterly,* No. 43, (July-September, 1970), pp. 47-80.
74. Murthy, T.S., "Military Factor in Sino-Inclian Talks," *Strategic Analysis,* Vol. 6, No. 12, March 1983, pp. 703-11.
75. "Tibet in Sino-Indian Relations: The Centrality of Marginality," *Asian Survey,* Vol. 37, No. 11, November 1997, pp. 1078-95.
76. Palmar, Norman D., "Trans-Himalayan Confrontation," *ORBIS,* VI (Winter, 1963), pp. 513-27.
77. Pradhan, Pradyot, "People's Republic of China: A Security Threat to India," *Strategic Analysis,* Vol. 11, No. 10, January 1988, pp. 1195-1210.
78. Rao, K. Krishna, "The Sino-Indian Boundary Question and International Law" *The International Law and Comparative Law Quarterly,* II, Part 2 (April, 1962), pp. 375-415.
79. Rubin, A.P., "The Sirio-Indian Border", *The International and Comparative Law Quarterly,* 9, Part 1 ( January, 1966), pp. 96-125.
80. "The Position of Tibet in International Law," *The China Quarterly,* VIII (July-September, 1968), pp. 110-54.
81. Satyapalan, G.N., "The Sino-Indian Border Conflict," *ORBIS,* VIII (Summer, 1964), pp. 374-90.
82. Sidky, Mohammad Habib, "Chinese World Strategy and South Asia:

The China Factor in Indo-Pakistani Relations," *Asian Survey,* Vol. 16, No. 10, October 1976, pp. 965-80.

83. "Sino-indian CBMs: Problems and Prospects," *Strategic Analysis,* Vol. 20, No. 4, July 1997, pp. 543-59.
84. Singh, Swaran, "Sino-Central Asian Ties," *IDSA Journal of Strategic Analysis,* New Delhi, September 2000.
85. Smith, Warren I., "Ideological Basis of China's Tibet Policy," *Tibetan Review,* Vol. 23, No. 11, November 1988, pp. 13-21.
86. Sreedhari, "China a Super Power?," *IDSA.journal of Strategic Analysis,* July 1997.
87. Stein, Arthur, "India's Relations with the USSR: 1953-1963," *ORBIS,* VIII (Summer, 1964), pp. 357-73.
88. Sun Zuangshi, "US Strategy in Central Asia," *Beijing Review,* Vol. 43, No. 26, June 26, 2000.
89. Swamy, Subramanian, "Economic Distance Between China and India, 1955-73," *China Quarterly,* Vol. 70, June 1977, pp. 371-83.
90. Vertzberger, Yaacov Y.I., "India's Strategic Posture and Border War Defeat of 1962: A Case Study in Miscalculation," *Journal of Strategic Studies,* Vol. 5, No. 3, September 1982.
91. Ward, Michael Don, and Mahajan, A.K., "Defense Expenditures, Security Threats and Governmental Deficits: A Case Study of India," *Journal of Conflict Resolution,* III (September, 1984), pp. 382-419. This article presents a model of defense spending in India based on empirical data.
92. Wang, Shaoguang, "Estimating China's Defence Expenditure," *China Quarterly,* 1996.
93. The Government of India, *Report of the Officials of the Governments of India and the People's Republic of China on the Boundary Question,* New Delhi: The Government of India Press, 1962.
94. *White Papers: Notes, Momoranda, Letters Exchanged Between the Governments of India and China,* 1954-64, Faridabad: The Government of India Press, Nos. I-IX.
95. The People's Republic of China: *Concerning the Question of Tibet,* Peking: Foreign Language Press, 1959.
96. *The Sino-Indian Border Question,* Peking: Foreign Language Press, 1962.

# APPENDIX I

# Home Minister Vallabhbhai Patel's Note to the Prime Minister

New Delhi: 7 November 1950

My dear Jawaharlal,

Ever since my return from Ahmedabad and after the Cabinet meeting the same day which I had to attend at practically 15 minutes' notice and for which I regret I was not able to read all the papers, I have been anxiously thinking over the problem of Tibet and I thought I should share with you what is passing through my mind.

2. I have carefully gone through the correspondence between the External Affairs Ministry and Our ambassador in Peking and through him the Chinese Government. I have tried to peruse this correspondence as favourably to our Ambassador and the Chinese Government as possible, but I regret to say that neither of them comes out well as a result of this study. The Chinese Government have tried to delude us by professions of peaceful intentions. My own feeling is that at crucial period they managed to instil into our Ambassador a false sense of confidence in their so-called desire to settle the Tibetan problem by peaceful means. There can be no doubt that during the period covered by this correspondence the Chinese must have been concentrating for an onslaught on Tibet. The final action of the Chinese, in my judgement, is little short of perfidy. The tragedy of it is that the Tibetans put faith in us; they chose to be guided by us and we have been unable to get them out of the meshes of Chinese diplomacy or Chinese malevolence. From the latest position, it appears that we shall not be able to rescue the Dalai Lama. Our Ambassador had been at great pains to find an explanation or justification for Chinese policy and actions. As the External Affairs Ministry remarked in one of their telegrams, there was a lack of firmness and unnecessary apology in one or two representations that he made to the Chinese Government on our behalf. It is impossible to imagine any sensible person believing in the so-called threat to China from Anglo-American mechanisation in Tibet. Therefore, if the Chinese put faith in this,

they must have distrusted us so completely as to have taken us as tools or stooges of Anglo-American diplomacy or strategy. This feeling, if genuinely entertained by the Chinese in spite of your direct approach to them, indicates that even though we regard ourselves as friends of China the Chinese do not regard us their friends. With the Communist mentality of 111-10e'v CI is not with them being against them," this is a significant pointer, of which we have to take due note. During the last several months, outside the Russian camp, we have practically been alone in championing the cause of Chinese entry into the UNO and in securing from the American assurances on the Formosa (now Taiwan) question. We have done everything we could to assuage Chinese feelings, to allay its apprehensions and to defend its legitimate claims in our discussions and correspondence with America and Britain and in the UNO. In spite of this, China is not concerned about our disinterestedness; it continued to regard us with suspicion and the whole psychology is one, at least outwardly, of scepticism, perhaps mixed with a little hostility. I doubt if we can go any further than we have done already to convince China of our good intentions, friendliness and goodwill. In Beijing we have an Ambassador who is eminently suitable for putting across the friendly point of view. Even he seems to have failed to convert the Chinese. Their last telegram to us is an act of gross discourtesy not only in the summary way it disposes of our protest against the entry of Chinese forces into Tibet but also in the wild insinuation that our attitude is determined by foreign influences. It looks as though it is not a friend speaking in that language but a potential enemy.

3. In the background of this, we have to consider what new situation now faces us as a result of the disappearance of Tibet, as we know it, and the expansion of China almost up to our gates. Throughout history we have seldom been worried about our north-east frontier. The Himalayas have been regarded as an impenetrable barrier against any threat from the north. We had a friendly Tibet which gave us no trouble. The Chinese were divided. They had their own domestic problems and never bothered us about our frontiers. In 1914, we entered into a convention with Tibet which was not endorsed by the Chinese. We seem to have regarded Tibetan autonomy as extending to independent treaty relationship. Pre-sumably, all that we required was Chinese counter-signature. The Chinese interpretation of suzerainty seems to be different. We can, therefore, safely assume that very soon they will disown all the stipulations which Tibet has entered into with us in the past. That throws into the melting pot all frontier and commercial settlements with Tibet on which we have been functioning and acting during the last half a century. China is no longer divided. It is united and strong. All

along the Himalayas in the north and north-east, we have on our side of the frontier a population ethnologically and culturally no different from Tibetans or Mongoloids. The undefined state of the frontier and the existence on our side of a population with its affinities to Tibetans or Chinese have all the elements of potential trouble between China and ourselves. Recent and bitter history also tells us that Communism is no shield against imperialism and that the Communists are as good or as bad imperialists as any other.

Chinese ambitions in this respect not only cover the Himalayan slopes on our side but also include important parts of They have their ambitions in Burma also. Burma has the added difficulty that it has no McMahon Line round which to build up even the semblance of an agreement. Chinese irredentism and Communist imperialism are different from the expansionism or imperialism of the Western Powers. The former has a cloak of ideology which makes it ten times more dangerous. In the guise of ideological expansion lie concealed racial, national or historical claims. The danger from the north and north-east, therefore, becomes both communist and imperialists. While our western and north-western threat to security is still as prominent as before, a new threat has developed from the north and north-east. Thus, for the first time, after centuries, India's defence has to concentrate itself on two fronts simultaneously. Our defence measures have so far been based on the calculations of a superiority over Pakistan. In our calculations we shall now have to reckon with Communist China in the north and in the north-east, a Communist China which has definite ambitions and aims and which does not, in any way, seen friendly disposed towards us.

4. Let us also consider the political conditions on those potentially troublesome frontier. Our northern or north-eastern approaches consist of Nepal, Bhutan, Sikkim, the Darjeeling (area) and tribal areas in Assam. From the point of view of communications, they are weak spots. Continuous defensive lines do not exist. There is almost an unlimited scope for infiltration. Police protection is limited to a very small number of passes. There, too, our outposts do not seem to be fully manned. The contact of these areas with us is by no means close and intimate. The people inhabiting these portions have no established loyalty or devotion to India. Even the Darjeeling and Kalimpong areas are not free from pro-Mongoloid prejudices. During the last three years we have not been able to make any appreciable approaches to the Nagas and other hill tribes in Assam. European missionaries and other visitors had been in touch with them, but their

influence was in no way friendly to India or Indians. In Sikkim, there was political ferment some time ago. It is quite possible that discontent is smouldering there. Bhutan is comparatively quiet, but its affinity with Tibetans would be a handicap. Nepal has a weak oligarchic regime based almost entirely on force; it is in conflict with a turbulent element of the population as well as with enlightened ideas of the modern age. In these circumstances, to make people alive to the new danger or to make them defensively strong is a very difficult task indeed and that difficulty can be got over only by enlightened firmness, strength and a clear line of policy. I am sure the Chinese and their sources of inspiration, Soviet Russia, would not miss any opportunity of exploiting these weak spots, partly in support of their ideology and partly in support of their ambitions. In my judgement, therefore, the situation is one in which we cannot afford either to be complacent or to be vacillating. We must have a clear idea of what we wish to achieve and also of the methods by which we should achieve it. Any faltering or lack of decisive-ness in formulating our objectives 01 in pursuing our policy to attain those objectives is bound to weaken us and increase the threats which are so evident.

5. Side by side with these external dangers, we shall now have to face serious internal problems as well. I have already asked (H.V.R.) Ienger to send to the E.A. Ministry a copy of the Intelligence Bureau's appreciation of these matters. Hitherto, the Communist Party of India had found some difficulty in contacting Communists abroad, or in getting supplies of arms, literature, etc. from them. They had to contend with the difficult Burmese and Pakistan frontiers on the east or with the long seaboard. They shall now have a comparatively easy means of access to Chinese Communists and through them to other foreign Communists. Infiltration of spies, fifth columnists and Communists would now be easier. Instead of having to deal with isolated Communist pockets in Telengana and Warangal we may have to deal with Communist arsenals in China. The whole situation thus raises a number of problems on which we must come to an early decision so that we can, as I said earlier. formulate the objectives of our policy and decide the methods by which those objectives are to be attained. It is also clear that action will have to be fairly comprehensive, involving not only our defence strategy and state of preparations but also problems of internal security to deal with which we have not a moment to lose. We shall also have to deal with administrative and political problems in the weak spots along the frontier to which I have already referred.

6. It is, of course, impossible for me to be exhaustive in setting out all these problems. I am, however, giving below some of the problems which, in

my opinion, require early solution and round which we- have to build our administrative or military policies and measures to implement them:

(a) A military and intelligence appreciation of the Chinese threat to India both on the frontier and to internal security.

(b) An examination of our military position arid such redisposition of our forces as might be necessary, particularly with the idea of guarding important routes or areas which are likely to be the subject of dispute.

(c) An appraisement of the strength of our forces and, if necessary, reconsideration of our retrenchment plans for the Army in the light of these new threats.

(d) A long-term consideration of our defence needs. My own feeling is that, unless we assure our supplies of arms, ammunition and armours, we should be making our defence position perpetually weak and we would not be able to stand up to the double threat of difficulties both from the west and north-west and north and north-east.

(e) The question of Chinese entry into UNO. In view of the rebuff which China has given us and the method which it has followed in dealing with Tibet. I am doubtful whether we can advocate its claims any longer. There would probably be a threat in the UNO virtually to outlaw China in view of its active participation in the Korean War. We must determine our attitude on this question also.

(f) The political and administrative steps which we should take to strengthen our northern and north-eastern frontiers. This would include the whole of the border, i.e. Nepal, Bhutan, Sikkim, Darjeeling and the tribal territory in Assam.

(g) Measures of internal security in the border areas as well as the states flanking those areas, such as UP, Bihar, Bengal and Assam.

(h) Improvement of our communications, road, rail, 'air and wireless, in these areas and with the frontier outposts.

(i) Policing and intelligence of frontier posts.

(j) The future of our mission at Lhasa and the trade posts at Gyantse and Yatung and the forces which we have in operation in Tibet to guard the trade routes.

(k) The policy in regard to the McMahon Line.

7. These are some of the questions which occur to my mind. It is possible that a consideration of these matters may lead us into wider questions of our relationship with China, Russia, America, Britain and Burma. This, however, would be of a general nature, though some might be basically very important, e.g. we might have to consider whether we should

not enter into closer association with Burma in order to strengthen the latter in its dealings with China. I do not rule out the possibility that, before applying pressure on us, China might apply pressure on Burma. With Burma, the frontier is entirely undefined and the Chinese territorial claims are more substantial. In its present position, Burma might offer an easier problem for China and, therefore, might claim its attention *(emphasis added)*.

8. I suggest that we meet early to have a general discussion on these problems and decide on such steps as we might think to be immediately necessary and direct quick examination of other problems with a view to taking early measures to deal with them.

Yours,
**Vallabhai Patel**

The Hon'ble Shri Jawaharlal Nehru
New Delhi.

[*Source.* (edited by Dr. S. Gopal), Sardar Patel's Correspondence, pp. 33541]

# APPENDIX II

# Prime Minister Jawaharlal Nehru's Note on China and Tibet

18 November, 1950

(The note was obviously forwarded to Sardar Patel as it answered indirectly some of the matters raised in the Patel's letter of 7 November 1950).

The Chinese Government having replied to our last note, we have to consider what further steps we should take in this matter. There is no immediate hurry about sending a reply to the Chinese Government. But we have to send immediate instructions to B.N. Rau as to what he should do in the event of Tibet's appeal brought up before the Security Council or the Central Assembly.

2. The content of the Chinese reply is much the same as their previous notes, but there does not appear to be a toning down and an attempt at some kind of a friendly approach.

3. It is interesting to note that they have not referred specifically to our mission Eat] Lhasa or to our trade agents or military escort at Gyantse etc. We had mentioned these especially in our last note. There is an indirect reference, however, in China's note. At the end, this note says that "As long as our two sides adhere strictly to the principle of mutual respect for territory, sovereignty, equality and mutual benefit, we are convinced that the friendship between China and India should be developed in a normal way and that problems relating to Sino-Indian diplomatic, commercial and cultural relations with respect to Tibet and to our trade agents and others in Tibet may be resolved. We had expected a demand from them for the withdrawal of these agents etc. The fact that they have not done so has some significance.

4. Stress is laid in China's note on Chinese sovereignty over Tibet, which we are reminded, we have acknowledged, on Tibet being an integral part of China's territory and therefore a domestic problem. It is however, again repeated that outside influences have been at play obstructing China's mission in 'Tibet'. In fact, it is stated that liberation of Changtu proves that

foreign forces and influences were inciting Tibetan troops to resist. It is again repeated that no foreign intervention will be permitted and that the Chinese army will proceed.

5. All this is much the same as has been said before, but it is said in a somewhat different way and there are repeated references in the note to China desiring the friendship of India.

6. It is true that in one of our messages to the Chinese government we used 'sovereignty' of China in relation to Tibet. In our last message we used the word "suzerainty." After receipt of the China's last note, we have pointed out to our Ambassador that "suzerainty" was the right word and that "sovereignty" had been used by error.

7. It is easy to draft a reply to the Chinese note, pressing our viewpoints and countering some of the arguments raised in the Chinese note. But before we do so we should be clear in our own minds as to what we are aiming at, not only in the immediate future but from a long-term view. It is important that we keep both these viewpoints before us. In all probability China, that is present-day China, is going to be our close neighbour for a long time to come. We are going to have a tremendously long common frontier. It is unlikely, and it would be unwise to expect, that the present Chinese government will collapse giving place to another. Therefore, it is important to pursue a policy which will be in keeping with this long-term view.

8. I think it may be taken for granted that China will take possession, in a political sense at least, of the whole of Tibet. There is no likelihood whatever of Tibet being able to resist this or stop it. It is equally unlikely that any foreign power can prevent it. We cannot do so. If so, what can we do to help in the maintenance of Tibetan autonomy and at the same time avoiding continuous tension and apprehension on our frontiers?

9. The Chinese note has repeated that they with the Tibetan people to have what they call "regional autonomy and religious freedom." This autonomy can obviously not be anything like the autonomy verging on independence which Tibet has enjoyed during the last forty years or so. But it is reasonable to assume from the very nature of Tibetan geography, terrain and climate, that a large measure of autonomy is almost inevitable. It may of course be that this autonomous Tibet is controlled by communist elements in Tibet. I imagine however that it is, on the whole, more likely that what will be attempted will be a pre-communist China administration rather than a communist one.

10. If world war comes, then all kinds of difficult and intricate problems arise and each one of these problems will be inter-related with others. Even

the question of defence of India assumes a different shape and cannot be isolated from other world factors. I think that is exceedingly unlikely that we may have to face any real military invasion from the Chinese side, whether in peace or in war, in the foreseeable future. I base this conclusion on a consideration of various world factors. In peace, such an invasion would undoubtedly lead to world war. China, though internally big, is in a way amorphous and easily capable of being attacked on its sea costs and by air. In such a war, China would have its main front in South and East and it will be fighting for its very existence against powerful enemies. It is inconceivable that it should divert its forces and its strength across the inhospitable terrain of Tibet and under-take a wild adventure across the Himalayas. Any such attempt will greatly weaken its capacity to meet its real enemies on other fronts. Thus I rule out any major attack on India by China. I think these considerations should be borne in mind, because there is far too much loose talk about China attacking and overriding India. If we lose our sense of perspective and world strategy and give way to unreasoning fears then any policy that we might have is likely to fail.

11. While there is, in any opinion, practically no chance of a major attack on India by China, there are certainly chances of gradual infiltration across our border and possibly of entering and taking possession of disputed territory, if there is no obstruction to this happening. We must therefore take all necessary precautions to prevent this. But again, we must differentiate between these precautions and those that might be necessary to meet a real attack.

12. If we really feared an attack and had to make full provision for it, this would cast an intolerable burden on us, financial and otherwise, and it would weaken our general defence position. There are limits beyond which we cannot go, at least for some years, and a spreading out of our army on distant frontiers would be bad from every military or strategic point of view.

13. In spite of our desire to settle the points at issue between us and Pakistan, and developing peaceful relations with it, the fact remains that our major possible enemy is Pakistan. This has compelled us to think of our defence mainly in terms of Pakistan's aggression. If we begin to think of, and prepare for China's aggression in the same way, we would weaken considerably on the Pakistan side. We might well be got in a pincer movement. It is interesting to note that Pakistan is taking a great deal of interest, from this point of view, in developments in Tibet. Indeed it has been discussed in the Pakistan Press that the new danger from Tibet to India might help them to settle the Kashmir problem according to their wishes.

Pakistan has absolutely nothing in common with China or Tibet. But if we fall out completely with China, Pakistan will undoubtedly try to take advantage of this, politically or otherwise. The position of India thus will be bad from a defence point of view. We cannot have all the time two possible enemies on either side of India. This danger will not be got over, even if we increase our defence forces or even if other foreign countries help us in arming. The measures of safety that one gets by increasing the defence apparatus is limited by many factors. But whatever that measures of safety might be, strategically we would be in an unsound position and the burden of this will be very great on us. As it is, we are facing enormous difficulties, financial, economic etc.

14. The idea that communism inevitably means expansion and war, or to put it more precisely, that Chinese communism means inevitably an expansion towards India, is rather naive.. It may mean that in certain circumstances. Those circumstances would depend upon many factors, which I need not go into here. The danger really is not from military invasion but from infiltration of men and ideas. The ideas are there already and can only be countered by other ideas. Communism is an important element in the situation. But, by our attaching too great importance to it in this context, we are likely to misjudge the situation from other and more important angles.

15. In a long-term view, India and China are two of the biggest countries of Asia bordering on each other and both with certain expansive tendencies, because of their vitality. If their relations are bad, this will have a serious effect not only on both of them but on Asia as a whole. It would affect our future for a long time. If a position arises in which China and India are inveterately hostile to each other, like France and Germany, then there will be repeated wars bringing destruction to both. The advantage will go to other countries. It is interesting to note that both the UK and the USA appear to be anxious to add to the unfriendliness of India and China towards each other. It is also interesting to find that USSR does not view with favour any friendly relations between India and China. These are long-term reactions which one can fully understand, because India and China, at peace with each other, would make a vast difference to the whole set-up and balance of the world. Much, of course, depends upon the development of either country and how far communism in China will mould the Chinese people. Even so, these processes are long-range ones and in the long run it is fairly safe to assume that hundred of millions of people will not change their essential characteristics.

16. These arguments lead to the conclusion that while we should be prepared, to the best of our ability, for all contingencies, the real protection that we should seek is some kind of understanding of China. If we have not got that, then both our present and our future are imperilled and no distant power can save us. I think on the whole that China desires this too for obvious reasons. If this is so, then we should fashion our present policy accordingly.

17. We cannot save Tibet, as we should have liked to do and our very attempts to save it might well bring greater trouble to it. It would be unfair to Tibet for us to bring this trouble upon her without having the capacity to help her effectively. It may be possible however that we might be able to help Tibet to retain a large measure of her autonomy. That would be good for Tibet and good for India. As far as I can see this can only be done on the diplomatic level and by avoidance of making the present tension between India and China worse.

18. When then should be our instructions to B.N. Rau? From the messages he has sent us, it appears that no member of the Security Council shows any inclination to sponsor Tibet's appeal and that there is a little likelihood of the matter being considered by the Council. We have said that [we] are not going to sponsor this appeal, but it - it comes up we shall state our viewpoint. This viewpoint cannot be one of full support of the Tibetan appeal, because that goes far and claims full independence. We may say that whatever might have been acknowledged in the past about China's sovereignty or suzerainty, recent events have deprived China of the right to claim that. There may be some moral basis for this argument. But it will not take us or Tibet very far. It will only hasten the downfall of Tibet. No outsiders will be able to help her and China, suspicious and apprehensive of these tactics, will make sure of much speedier and fuller possession of Tibet than she might otherwise have done. We shall thus not only fail in our endeavour but at the same time have really hostile China on our doorstep.

19. I think that in no event should we sponsor Tibet's appeal. I would personally think that it would be a good thing if that appeal is not heard in the Security Council of the General Assembly. If it is considered there, there is bound to be a great deal of bitter speaking and accusation, which will worsen the situation as regards Tibet, as well as the possibility of widespread war, without helping it in the least. It must be remembered that neither the UK nor the USA, nor indeed any other power is particularly interested in Tibet or the future of that country. What they are interested in is embarrassing China. Our interest, on the other hand, is Tibet, and if we cannot serve that interest, we fail. (emphasis added)

20. Therefore, it will be better not to discuss Tibet's appeal in the UN. Suppose, however, that it comes up for discussion, in spite of our not wishing this, what then? I would suggest that our representative should state our case as moderately as possible and ask the Security Council or the Assembly to give expression to their desire that the Sino-Tibetan question should be settled peacefully and that Tibet's autonomy should be respected and maintained. Any particular reference to an article of the Charter of the UN might tie us up in the difficulties and lead to certain consequences later, which may prove highly embarrassing for us. Or a resolution of the UN might just be a dead letter, which also will be bad.

21. If my general argument is approved, then we can frame our reply to China's note accordingly.

J. NEHRU

18 November 1950

(Source: Dr. S. Gopal: Sardar Patel's Correspondence, pp. 342-47).

# Appendix III

# "We Face Common Problems" Deng Xiaoping in a meeting with Dr. Subramanian Swamy in Beijing on April 8, 1981

Dr. Subramanian Swamy, 41, the Janata Party MP, was back in the head-line-grabbing business following his historic 100-minute interview with Chinese strongman Deng Xiaoping in Beijing's Great Hall of the People. Deng is vice-chairman of the Communist Party of China and currently the most powerful man in Beijing. His remarks on improving Sino-Indian relations are the first such high level statements since the diplomatic freeze between the two countries following India's recognition of the Heng Samrin regime in Kampuchea last year.

China, for Swamy, has been familiar ground. This was his third visit to China since 1978 and though he was not an official emissary of the Government, the presence of the Indian ambassador in Beijing, S.K. Bajpai, at the interview, elevated the meeting to an inter-governmental communication. Swamy agreed to give India Today exclusive rights to the full transcript of his meeting with Deng, which is reproduced below.

**Swamy:** It is great honour for me to meet a great leader of China. I have been your admirer for 15 years.

**Deng:** Well, this year you are 41. You are in the prime of life. Me, I am already very old.

**Swamy:** You look very young. It is like my party's former prime minister Morarji Desai. He is 85 but acts younger than I.

**Deng:** I have never met Morarji Desai but I would like you to give him my regards.

**Swamy:** Thank you. Excellency, in the last few years there has been a good development of our relations but we are countries with such a long history, and with so much that need our cooperation, it pains me if we do not have the greatest of friendship. I hope that we can develop this much more.

**Deng:** Yes, we are two big countries. We have had over 2,000 years of good relations and we should have more friendship and cooperation. We have both had great civilisations. We have also had common misfortunes. India was a colonial country and we were semi-colonial. Now we are the two biggest countries in the world. If our two populations were put together it could come to more than one-third of the world but when we talk of ourselves as big countries what do we mean?

Really just that we have these big populations. We are also poor countries. We face common problems. India is a Third World country, so is China. It is necessary for us to work together. In the early '50s we had very close friendship. Premier Chou En-lai visited India and had a very good visit. Later on Prime Minister Nehru came to China. Then in the late '50s problems developed between us. We had this long period of strain. After that we started to normalise relations.

Actually, what do we mean by this word normalisation? We already have ambassadors in both countries so in that sense relations are normal. However, if we mean that we should have more friendship then certainly that is correct. There is no reason why we should not improve our relations and no reason why we should not have more exchanges between us. This has always been my view. Even when I went to Nepal I said so and in fact there was some positive response from your side to my statement. Even earlier the late Chairman Mao Zedong was of the same view. I recall that he spoke to your charge d'affaires and then we started trying to improve our relations. Your foreign minister paid us a visit. There have been all these twists and turns in our relations. We even had to postpone the visit of our Foreign Minister Huang Hua. However, it is necessary to work for better relations and we have decided that Huang Hua will visit India soon.

**Swamy:** I am very glad to hear that Foreign Minister Huang Hua will be visiting us soon. You may be sure lie will be given a warm welcome. Actually, the people of India have very warm feelings for China and visitors from China are made welcome. Even the groups—we just had some acrobats who were very well received and you will find that your foreign minister will have nothing but affection from the people of India. They will give him good reception as I am sure the Government of India also will.

**Deng:** Your Prime Minister Mrs Gandhi was good enough to receive our acrobats. Please thank her for this.

**Swamy:** Certainly. But you know, Excellency, this has been said before—the Xinhua commentary of last June made the point that the only real outstanding problem between us is the border question. Once that is solved then all questions between us can go and we can really develop our relations into the best of friendship. What is your view on this border issue, how can we solve it?

**Deng:** Our position on this is very clear. Not only our news papers but that is the position of the Government that if we both approach the problem with understanding there will be no difficulty in reaching a solution through repeated discussions. There is my own proposal for a package deal. Until that can be settled let us develop contacts in other fields. Then there is this question of threat. Some people talk of threat in India, that there is a threat from China and in China that there is a threat from India. How can there be any threat. There is the whole Tibetan Plateau between us. There is very little oxygen and it is not even possible to deploy a large number of troops. From the beginning of the People's Republic of China (PRC) we have hardly any troops near you. We can never be a threat to you nor do we think you are a threat to us. Actually, we are told that you have many more troops on your side of the border than we have on ours but that does not make you a threat.

Even if you were to take part of Tibet, that would not be a threat to China. It is not India by itself that could be a threat. What we consider a danger is that some other force may take a hand there. The real threat is from the North. There are a million troops deployed there. Moreover, the Soviet Union is instigating Vietnam to make it a threat from the South.

**Swamy:** I entirely agree with you but you know there is one problem—people in India wonder—you know in all the years after our crisis, inspite of our differences India never changed its position: whether on your admission to the United Nations, whether on Taiwan question, whether on Tibet, the Indian position was to support you completely but on your side statements used to be made—all sorts of things are said and our public wonders about your wanting to be friends; so some sort of gesture would be useful. On Sikkim for instance why can't you accept that it is part of India. As to the way it happened—our former prime minister, Morarji Desai has said he did like the way it was done but he also made it clear these things are irreversible. India is a merger of states and once merged: nothing can be done. I ask because your maps show it separate and so questions are asked by people in India that you do not want our relations to improve. The Soviet lobby is very active—every day the Soviet Union has it in papers that we should not trust you, that you are too clever and will fool us. There are so many planted stories. So if you do not recognise the position on Sikkim, there are many people who take advantage of this whereas if you were to recognise it, it would be a good gesture of your intentions and it would help people like me who want to advocate friendship with China.

**Deng:** On Sikkim our position is very clear. We made an official statement at the time of annexation that we could not accept annexation. We disapprove because it is contrary both to international norms and to morality. We will not change our position on this. Indeed, there is no reason why ·we should change our position. We can never approve of the annexation. However, we have also said that we will not mention or make use of the subject when discussing Sino-Indian relations. Actually, I told this both to a journalist from India and to your Foreign Secretary, Gonsalves, when he came here. I repeat again we will not mention or make use of this subject in discussing the improvement of Sino-Indian relations. It is important that we improve our bilateral relations. We have to take note of the situation in the world and act in the larger context.

**Swamy:** I believe that when President zia-ul-I-Iaq of Pakistan was here last year, he had said to you that he would like to improve relations with India. Actually, there was some progress. Our ambassador here used to be ambassador in Pakistan and I know he did a very good job. It is very necessary for us to have good relations with Pakistan. Lately there have been some hold ups. I mention our Sino-Indian bilateral relations because of the importance I attach to friendship but I agree with you that it is not only our bilateral relations, it is our relations with neighbours and the position of China and India in the subcontinent and in Asia as a whole that are important. I wonder if you could comment on how we could bring about better relations in the subcontinent and what China could do in that context.

**Deng:** It is certainly very important that you improve your relations with your neighbours. They worry about you. It is not only Pakistan, there is Nepal, there is Bangladesh, even Sri Lanka. We know these countries. We have contact with them and we hear their views about you and their relations with you. There is Bhutan also. We do not know very much about Bhutan but generally, where your neighbours are concerned you are so big and they are so small. Actually in the subcontinent you are the big brother. The big brother has to show more understanding of the smaller.

**Swamy:** I agree with you entirely that you know these neighbours. When you have a smaller neighbour there are problems. You have neighbour Vietnam which is very afraid of you. Would you tell me how you think you could improve relations with Vietnam?

**Deng:** As regards Vietnam I do not think you are well informed. We could not understand their attitude towards us. Look at it from the very beginning China had excellent relations. We helped them all along first in their struggle against the colonial masters France then during their war. with America. We were a poor country—we are a poor country—but we tighten our belts and gave them everything we could, even if we had to do without things. Actually we gave them over 20 billion dollars worth of help. We could not understand why they turned against us. Soviet Union has instigated them. They are an Ungrateful nation. But that would not matter.

When Cambodia was having to fight its war against imperialists we also have had to help Cambodia. We have no common border with Cambodia. Everything we sent had to go through Vietnam then we found they were taking it themselves. Nothing that we sent reached the Cambodia. The greedy Vietnamese were keeping it all even though that meant denying help to our friends in Cambodia. 'I-he Russians have been at work and the leadership in Vietnam has been instigated by Russians to be a threat to us. We were very patient but everyday there were provocations. Finally, we decided we had to teach them a lesson. I said this when I was in America. Carter did not like it. He did not approve but we said it had to be done. We have no enmity against Vietnam but when they behaved like that it was necessary to teach them a lesson so we sent our forces and after we have taught them a lesson that they could not behave like that then we withdrew our forces.

Actually on this there was a lot of questioning because it happened when your foreign minister was here and you all said why did you not tell us in advance. The fact is we forgot about it. We had been saying it for so many months we thought everybody knew. There was no secret. We had said so many times. I can assure you there was no intention on our part to do it while your foreign minister was here. It just happened but we had no aggressive intentions towards Vietnam. We would like friendship but they did not allow it.

**Swamy:** In regard to the international situation, would you say that the danger of war has increased? The situation in Poland is very worrying. The Soviet Union has already moved into Afghanistan and there is this danger now in Poland. You used to say that another world was is inevitable but do you think the danger had increased?

**Deng:** Certainly there is great danger but we do not think it necessary to say that it is immediate and that it does not have to happen now. However, if it is to be delayed we have to be vigilant. The first two world wars started over small things. Whether it is Afghanistan, whether it is Poland we have to be vigilant, whether these are beginnings of other things.

**Swamy:** Thank you. You are a very busy man. You have very important responsibilities but I would like to just ask three more questions. First, your relations with the United States. How do you view them?

**Deng:** With the United States there is no reason, from the beginning, why we should not be friends except Taiwan and their two China theory. If they do this, it will not only put an end to progress in Sino-US relations, it would be a retrogression. We have made this clear to the Americans. We have spoken to them many times and said that we would like to be friends but this is one matter which we cannot stand. They have assured us that they have no such intention. They too have talked to us. We have said what about Reagan's campaign speeches? They have said his campaign speeches were only for the campaign and that is now over. However, we must remember the Reagan Administration is less than three months in office and we should wait and see whether its foreign policy stabilises.

**Swamy:** What about Sino-USSR relations? You said that the danger is from the North and I agree with you but do you see any possibility of your improving relations with the Russians?

**Deng:** As for improving relations with the USSR, there is nothing in the way if the USSR gives up liege monism. That is what has caused the problem with us and with other countries. We could be friends easily if they were to give up their hegemonism but is it possible to imagine that? Their policy is that of the Czars. Actually, that was the problem. We wanted to improve relations and we started having talks with them but then they moved into Afghanistan and we had to break off the talks. They behave as expansionists. They have been instigating Vietnam as I have already told you. Then there is their action in Afghanistan. You know this is an attempt to get to the Indian Ocean. Actually, this is a matter for you to worry about the Russians always tried to use others even the war between China and India. Khrushchev visited India in 1959 and what developed from that. It is Soviet hegemonism that is the danger and it is for your country to consider it also.

**Swamy:** I again agree entirely with you, but to change to another subject. You have lately been laying stress—you have moved away from earlier emphasis on heavy industry and have been stressing the need to develop light industry and provide more consumer goods for your people. There is this readjustment going on. Is this a permanent shift in your economic strategy or is this emphasis on light industry only for a short period?

**Deng:** This is while we complete our readjustment. The fact is that we have made mistakes from the beginning and we find we have gone wrong because we started the wrong way. We now have to start again and we find we have made other mistakes. So it is necessary for us to look carefully and made the necessary readjustments but our present approach is for this period of readjustment.

**Swamy:** One last question. Excellency, you are good enough to note that I am still young. I would like to develop my political career and serve my people in the years to come. You have done so much—as I said I have been your admirer for the last 15 years—is there any advice you would give me?

**Deng:** The only thing that I can say is that I have always been an optimist. Even when things were going wrong I have remained an optimist and I have always been right. When I look back I think one should be calm and never give up. I remain an optimist also about our relations.

**Swamy:** Thank you, I must remember that.

**Deng:** (starting to get up). Thank you for your visit.

**Bajpai:** Excuse me. I do not wish to delay you Vice-Chairman but I would like to say a few words.

**Deng:** Please.

**Bajpai:** I did not wish to intervene before because this is Dr Swamy's day. It is his call on you and I am here by courtesy. Actually, I have just returned from Delhi and I have already spoken Io your Foreign Office that 1 had an opportunity to talk with my leaders and in the light of my discussions I hope to call on the leaders here in due course. I hope that some clay soon I can call on your excellency and perhaps I can then discuss some of these matters more fully. At the moment I would not go into details but I am bound to say that on a number of formulations the Government of India would agree with either of you—your excellency or Dr Swamy—whether it is what you said about Sikkin or when you referred to an unfortunate period of our relations with you and to our being egged on by Khruschev.

I have been most encouraged by many of your remarks and by your basic approach that you would like to see further improvement of relations with India. That is also the policy of the Government of India and we would like to see further improvement of relations with China but if you are going to have misconceptions about us—if for example you assume that India can be instigated in a particular policy by another country then I am afraid the task of improving relations becomes very much more difficult. I think we have both to realise that we are each sovereign independent countries and just as you take your decisions on the basis of your own judgement and analysis.

India also decides for itself. If misconceptions to the contrary persist then as I say it becomes much more difficult to improve relations. If, however, we respect each other's independence of judgement and action then I am sure the Government of India would share the optimism you have expressed just as we share the desire for improvement of relations.

**Deng:** That is all right—it does not matter if we do not agree on some points.

INDIA TODAY
May 1-15, 1981

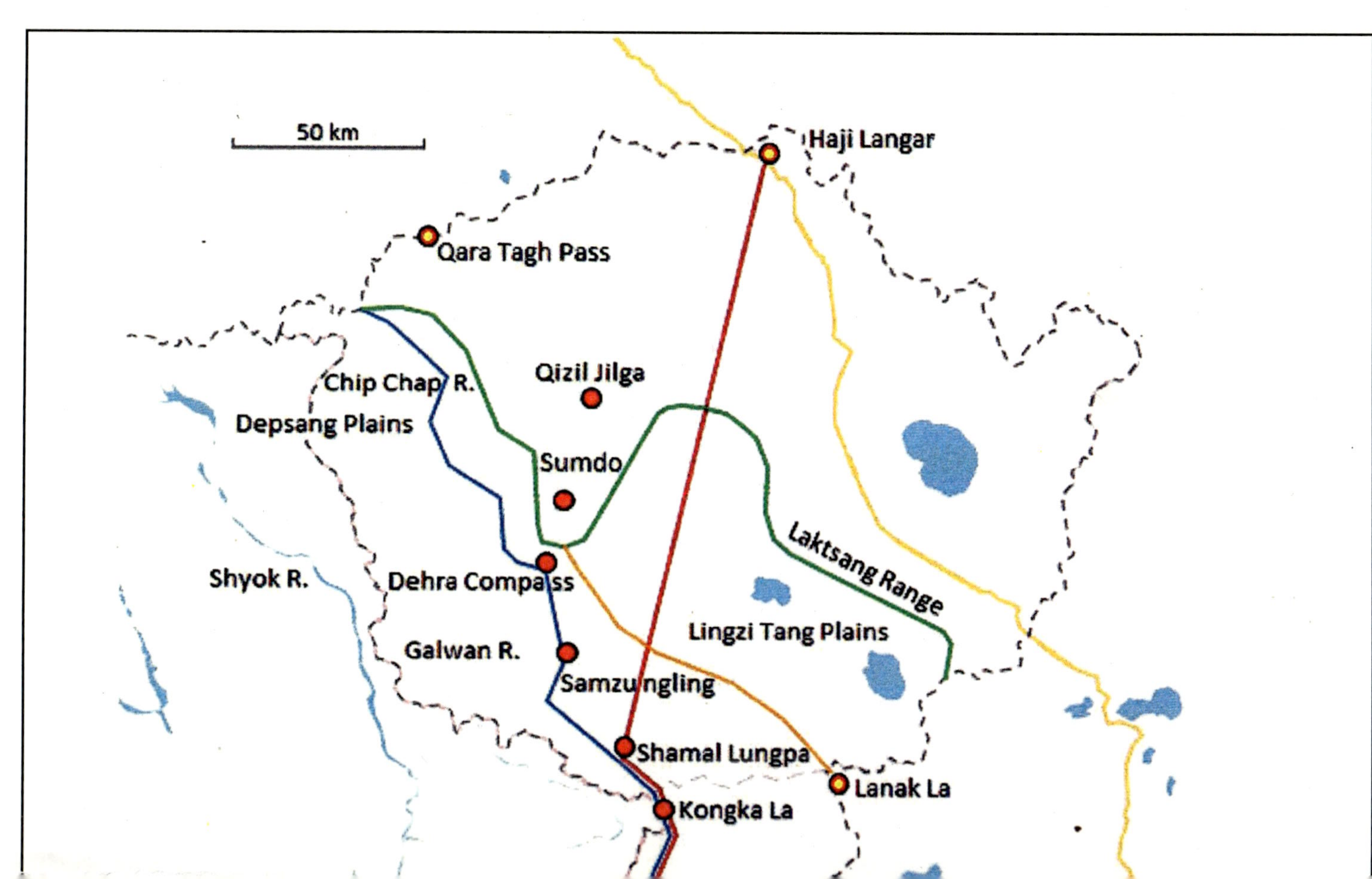
50 km
Haji Langar
Qara Tagh Pass
Qizil Jilga
Chip Chap R.
Depsang Plains
Sumdo
Laktsang Range
Shyok R.
Dehra Compass
Lingzi Tang Plains
Galwan R.
Samzungling
Shamal Lungpa
Lanak La
Kongka La